The Black Power Mixtape, 1967–1975
by Göran Hugo Olsson

Haymarket Books
PO Box 180165
Chicago, IL 60626
773-583-7884
info@haymarketbooks.org
www.haymarketbooks.org

ISBN: 978-1-60846-296-4

Trade distribution:
In the US, Consortium Book Sales and Distribution, www.cbsd.com
In Canada, Publishers Group Canada, www.pgcbooks.ca
In the UK, Turnaround Publisher Services, www.turnaround-uk.com
In Australia, Palgrave Macmillan, www.palgravemacmillan.com.au
All other countries, Publishers Group Worldwide, www.pgw.com

Cover and inlay design by Stefania Malmsten and Jonas Bard

Published with the generous support of Lannan Foundation and the Wallace Global Fund.

Printed in the United States by union labor.
Library of Congress cataloging-in-publication data is available.

10 9 8 7 6 5 4 3 2 1

The Black Power Mixtape 1967–1975

by Göran Hugo Olsson

Haymarket Books
Chicago, Illinois

Anybody can die nobly for a cause.
The sign of maturity is to live
day by day for that cause.
It is not a racial cause.
It is here, but somewhere else
it's a religious cause.
But it's really simple freedom.

—Melvin Van Peebles, 2010

Preface
Danny Glover
San Francisco, 2013

The Black Power Mixtape, 1967–1975 is an extraordinary window into the Black freedom struggle in the United States, offering a treasure trove of fresh archival information about the Black Power movement and vivid portraits of some of its most dynamic participants, including Angela Davis and Stokely Carmichael.

The film—and this book—bring to life this incredible moment in our history, one which people know far too little about and which has profound relevance for our own time. We have much to learn from these visionary organizers who sought to redefine and reimagine democracy, whose sense of empowerment derived from the belief that the people could be the architects for change.

The Swedish film crews whose footage is featured in *The Black Power Mixtape* were able to capture this energy on camera in part because they came to this movement from the outside looking in. They asked sometimes very innocent yet illuminating questions, such as one posed to Angela Davis. Asked about her views on violence, she responds, "You ask me, you know, whether I approve of violence—I mean, that just doesn't make any sense at all. . . . I just find it incredible, because what it means is that the person who's asking that question has absolutely no idea what Black people have gone through, what Black people have experienced in this country, since the time the first Black person was kidnapped from the shores of Africa."

As Paul Robeson said, each generation makes its own history. A new generation must now make its history, but it faces huge challenges, whether it's the climate crisis, the global financial crisis, the crisis of poverty, or the crisis of inequity in the world. But we don't have to start anew. All of us can draw on the immense resources of those who struggled before us. And the people in *The Black Power Mixtape, 1967–1975* gave us strong shoulders to stand on.

Introduction
Göran Hugo Olsson
Stockholm, 2013

Some years ago I was walking home from work. It was late and the snow was melting as it fell. I was sad. Standing in the dark on the pavement outside the Ringen shopping mall, one of the most depressing places in Stockholm, I realized that it was only thanks to the music in my earphones that I was still functioning. This sound literally saving my mental health was an album by the Philadelphia soul legend Billy Paul, produced by the geniuses Gamble and Huff. The mix of lush soundscapes and social consciousness gave me both comfort and motivation. To show my gratitude, I decided that night to make a film about Billy Paul.

One of the key decisions in that project was that every scene was to be shot at night. I generally detest whitewashed, bland images taken in daylight. So in addition to my own filming, I looked for archive footage captured after dark in the late sixties and seventies. The problem was that the material had not been indexed in terms of daylight or night, so I had to sit down and watch every single foot of film shot in the United States that had been collected in Swedish archives.

But in the back of my mind was also a rumor, originating from older filmmakers, that Sweden had more footage on the Black Panthers than the United States did—which I found hard to believe. So I started spending time in the archive of the old Swedish Television (now Sveriges Television). I struck gold very quickly. On one of my first days of research, I discovered both a speech by Stokely Carmichael and a jailhouse interview with Angela Davis, and I was blown away by what I saw. Together those pieces make up the cornerstones of the film. They gave me the idea to make a film depicting the struggle of Black America in the late sixties and early seventies. There was a story there, in between the black-and-white footage of the optimistic Stokely in his sharp suits and full-color Angela in her bell-bottoms and trademark Afro facing a death penalty conviction.

One of the reasons this film works is that it has such a distinct perspective. As the captions state in the very first frame of the film: "This film consists of footage shot by Swedish reporters 1967–1975. It does not presume to tell the whole story of the Black Power movement, but rather to show how it was perceived by some Swedish filmmakers."

As an outsider, you could ask stupid or even arrogant-sounding questions and still get great answers. People understand that you do not have the language or the American experience because you are from this remote country close to the North Pole. And so they try to explain, to enlighten you. Everyone interviewed in this project has been so generous and forthcoming in helping us outsiders to understand. I think that both the original filmmakers and I have benefited tremendously from this generosity.

I wanted the film to be "Swedish" in tone—but it's not so easy to say what "Swedish" means. I use it in this context almost as a joke, referring to long-gone prejudices about how Swedes were or saw themselves or behaved in the world; with a consciousness, a strong sense of justice, not seldom at the expense of being boring.

At the same time I also understood the importance of having trustworthy Americans on board who both knew the American experience and had a feel for the cinematic. I was told that Danny Glover's production company, Louverture Films, was doing interesting work. We literally knocked on the door to their office in New York City and Danny's production partner, Joslyn Barnes, answered. I told her we had a film that we wanted them to coproduce. Joslyn was polite, but she did let me know: that's not the way it works here. Maybe in Sweden, but here you can't just knock on someone's door and assume you'll get a meeting. But somehow I managed to get her to sit down and let me show her a few clips. She said, "This is great, you have to talk to Danny. He's in Sweden, by the way." So the producer Annika Rogell, my son John, and I went to see Danny at his hotel a week later. He welcomed us to his suite and we talked for an hour and a half, mostly—and strangely—about the difference in the economies of Angola and Mozambique. And that was it.

I think this film shows some of the most brilliant and inspiring minds of their time. You might agree or disagree with the views of Stokely Carmichael or Angela Davis. But what everyone has to acknowledge is the impact this movement had in developing justice, democracy, and the way we see ourselves. I think of democracy not as a steady state, but as something that has to develop and evolve constantly. It's like boiling water: one has to expend energy under the pot all the time in order to keep the water cooking. And this movement did really put energy into the process of democracy and the development of freedom, not only for people of color in America or minorities all over the world but for all individuals. We all benefit from the labor and sacrifices made by these extraordinary people and this very important movement.

The film *The Black Power Mixtape, 1967–1975* has been released in cinemas in twenty-two countries, including the United States, the United Kingdom, France, Germany, and Sweden. One of the questions I am most frequently asked while promoting the film is: Why did filmmakers and reporters from remote Sweden create this material?

Of course there is no single answer to that, but it is amazing how much Sweden did broadcast on this subject. Angela Davis was almost a household name in Sweden in the early seventies.

The connection goes back in time, but it was sparked when Dr. Martin Luther King Jr. received the Nobel Peace Prize in 1964. We have reason to believe that the mind behind his nomination was Gunnar Myrdal, who briefly appears in the film alongside Dr. King, Coretta Scott King, Harry Belafonte, and the king of Sweden. Myrdal was a Swedish professor of economics who wrote the pioneering book *An American Dilemma: The Negro Problem and Modern Democracy in 1944*. In his book, Myrdal predicted the obstacles to full participation of the "American Negroes" in American society and had a great impact on how racial issues were viewed in the United States.

I think one could therefore say that awarding Dr. King the Nobel connected the Swedish establishment to the US civil rights movement. That connection was extended by the Swedish generation that coalesced around the events of May 1968, picking up the concept of Black Power along the way. Students invited activists like Stokely Carmichael and Bobby Seale to lecture at universities and student unions.

Another reason for Swedish interest in the injustices of the United States was the war in Vietnam. Not only did a majority of young Swedes support the struggle of the people of Vietnam against the US forces, but even at the highest levels of Swedish government there were great concerns about the war. This conflict came to a head in 1972, when Prime Minister Palme compared the bombings of Hanoi to the war crimes of Nazi Germany, resulting in the US ambassador withdrawing from Sweden. This was at the peak of the Cold War. Neutral Sweden became a sanctuary for many American soldiers, many of them Black, who deserted from airbases in Germany on their way to Vietnam. By the end of the sixties there were not a lot of African Americans in the streets of Sweden, but the ones who did find their way here were pretty well taken care of and often regarded as heroes. This stands in stark and sad contrast to the situation in Sweden today, where many refugees are looked upon with mistrust.

Sweden, being a homogeneous, neutral, and rich country, decided to produce its own news media instead of depending on French, American, or—God forbid—Soviet media. Swedes were sent all over the planet to tell their fellow countrypeople about the world in an endless chain of news stories and documentaries. Nonetheless, the audience didn't exactly have freedom of choice, dependent as they were on only two public-service channels available at the time.

New technology also played a role. Before 1967, most, if not all, reports from the United States were related by telephone by a senior Swedish editor, overlaid onto grainy newsreels from the big American agencies. New, lightweight equipment enabled a younger generation to use these powerful tools to create more in-depth, sophisticated television.

In addition to these images and voices from the past, we recorded contemporary reflections to put the events into their historical context—an idea that came from Danny in the very first moment of our unforgettable brainstorming meeting in Malmö. I remember stumbling out from his hotel with the words *put into context, put into context* spinning in my mind.

It was, however, very important for me not make a film full of "talking heads" shots of people telling their views on history. I wanted this fantastic archival footage to shine from beginning to end. I had another influence as well. A great joy for me, and for many of my colleagues, is watching DVDs with the audio commentary track on. That gave me the idea to try to make the film feel a bit like an audio commentary track, putting the events on screen into context and perspective.

The process of choosing which voice to record was a very organic one. At the time I was living in Brooklyn, working in our small living room. There I edited one sequence and asked myself and my producers: "Who could comment on this?" The selection process was, for me, based on trust.

I brought in people I knew, not always personally, but from their work. I knew Erykah Badu and Talib Kweli from their work and trusted their opinions—not to mention the great Harry Belafonte, a true hero. And the list goes on and on. One of the key people in giving us perspective was Sonia Sanchez, an amazing poet and person, whom I met in her gracious home in the Germantown section of Philadelphia.

I normally showed each person the footage on my computer for them to comment on during or after watching each clip. This was, of course, very inspiring and encouraging for me, since all of the commentators were totally fascinated by the material and surprised that Swedes had produced it. The most exciting moment was the afternoon I spent with Professor Angela Davis, browsing through the extra material we had on her, most notably her jailhouse interview. Drinking tea in my hotel room in Berkeley and talking with Angela Davis about this and many other things was truly a highlight of my professional life.

In selecting voices, we always tried to get different perspectives. After recording Angela Davis and Sonia Sanchez, we felt that the film needed a younger male voice, and that was Talib. We needed a younger female voice and so we brought in Erykah. But it wasn't just a question of perspective. It was also about trying to create dynamics in the sound of the film.

A common problem in working with archival film is that, no matter how sparkling the material, after a while the audience begins to feel claustrophobic. The material locks them in a fixed place in time and space. A filmmaker can add fresh oxygen into that container by bringing in new voices that complements the footage, making it easier for the audience to stay with the story. Another element that can serve this purpose is graphics. Ours, created by the wizard Stefania Malmsten, avoid the usual retro pitfalls and mediate a contemporary and fresh take on the subject that still evinces a deep sense of heritage. Stefania's graphics were also in line with the general attempt of the film to be correct, informative, respectful, and beautiful. The same can be said of the music, created by Ahmir-Khalib "Questlove" Thompson and Om'Mas Keith, curated by Corey Smyth. It's impossible to overstate how important the music is to this film.

This book is based on the material that made up the film *The Black Power Mixtape, 1967–1975*. Of course, only a fraction of the recorded material made it into the film. Publishing a book is an attempt to let some of the great things that had to be left out of the film become public.

About the Author

Göran Hugo Olsson is an award-winning documentary filmmaker. His film The Black Power Mixtape 1967–1975 *opened at the Sundance Film Festival 2011 and has played at cinemas in more than twenty-five countries. Olsson is a co-founder of the production outfit Story in Stockholm, Sweden. He also writes and teaches.*

MALCOLM X 1925-1965
ALCOLM X 1925-1965

Contributors

This book consists of voices recorded by Swedish reporters between 1967 and 1975. As with the film, it does not presume to tell the whole story of the Black Power movement, but rather to show how it was perceived by some Swedish filmmakers.

Literally hundreds of people worked to collect this unique material. The index cards in the archives do not always tell who produced the films and inserts. The cinematographers, in particular, often go unmentioned. The most frequent contributors are: Ingrid Dahlberg and the late Lars Hjelm, rest in peace, who did the important film on Stokely Carmichael. Christian Stanow and Göran Bengtsson made the beautiful prologue from Hallandale. Raija Lounavaara interviewed Bobby Seale. One of the cornerstones of this film is the entirely unique interview with Angela Davis in prison, conducted and produced by Bo Holmström, the Swedish correspondent to the United States at the time. He also contributed to many other parts of the film, including, most remarkably, the piece on the impoverished family in Brooklyn, which we paired with the vocals of Erykah Badu in the film. Not only did he report from the United States during this pivotal time, he was also covering the famine in Biafra and presenting shows in Sweden. Studying the files in the archive you could track his movements almost day by day, traveling from the East Coast to California, then to Africa, followed by a week of studio-produced television in Stockholm. Bo Holmström is a hard-hitting reporter and a master of the art of the follow-up question—in contrast to the other Swedes, who worked more in a "filmmaker" style. Much of the material from Harlem was taken from a two-piece television show called *Harlem Voices* that was more than three hours long, made by the veteran television producers Lars Ulvenstam and Tomas Dillén, with the late, profoundly talented Anders Ribsjö on camera. Interestingly enough, the Harlem native Tony Miller served as both sound technician and guide. Toward the end of the film he can be seen taking sound and directing people on the streets of Harlem.

Örjan Öberg did the fabulous piece on *TV Guide*'s articles on Swedish anti-Americanism, as well as the interview with the ever-so-brilliant Emile de Antonio. Other contributors include John Sune Carlson, Lars Helander, Bertil Askelöf, Sven Anér, Sid Birchman, Tom Goetz, Nils Åke Hamberg, Lars Hellengren, Bo Holmqvist, Bo Isaksson, Owe Johansson, Michael Kimmanson, Ingmar Odlander, Lars B. Pettersson, Jonas Sima, Knut Ståhlberg, Lars Tjernberg, and Anders Turai. Mats Nileskär recorded the radio interview with Abiodun Oyewole, which was not only brilliant but also served as a very important inspiration for the overall design of the film.

The commentators who were so forthcoming and generous to the project are some of the very finest artists and activists in America: Erykah Badu, Talib Kweli, Harry Belafonte, Kathleen Cleaver, Angela Davis, Robin D. G. Kelley, Abiodun Oyewole, Melvin Van Peebles, Sonia Sanchez, Bobby Seale, Questlove, and Kenny Gamble.

This book is truly a collective work by so many great people who have worked hard—and sometimes even risked their own lives—to tell the world these stories. Many of them remain unidentified. So instead of dividing the fees into hundreds of fractions, we have decided to donate royalties from this book to the Algebra Project. Those contributors who have publishing deals have been particularly gracious in this regard.

The Algebra Project was founded by the civil rights hero Bob Moses. It is a national nonprofit organization that uses mathematics as an organizing tool to ensure quality public-school education for every child in America. The Algebra Project is premised on the idea that every child has a right to a quality education, to succeed in this technology-based society, and to exercise full citizenship, and seeks to achieve this by using educational and research best practices and by building coalitions to create systemic change. You can learn more about the Algebra Project at www.algebra.org.

Prelude

Christian Stanow Reporter, Swedish Television

Hallandale, Florida, 1972

CHRISTIAN STANOW: And on the other side of the ocean, they came upon a beach. It was not, however, the Spice Coast that they had initially been seeking. But that did not make such a difference after all.

They called the country America. Built houses, hoisted flags, exterminated Indians. They had a revolution and freed themselves from the Old World's oppression.

With a foundation of new societal values and enormous natural resources, the USA quickly became the world's richest nation. Industrialism rolled out over the continent and took possession of it.

The Declaration of Independence, from 1776, is one of humanity's most important documents. With force, it decrees that "all men are created equal," that they "are endowed by their Creator with certain unalienable Rights, that among these are Life, Liberty and the pursuit of Happiness."

An enormous bulldozer drowns the ocean's roar with its relentless rumble. The seashore is in Hallandale, a few miles north of Miami, Florida. For the sake of tourists and the economy, they try to keep the sand cleansed of the oil and tar that the Atlantic's swell brings ashore daily.

Fair-skinned, a bit starry-eyed, perhaps, and very Swedish, we disembarked on this shore in the spring of 1972. We wanted to understand and portray America through sound and image—as it really is. However, there are about as many opinions on that as there are Americans: 210 million.

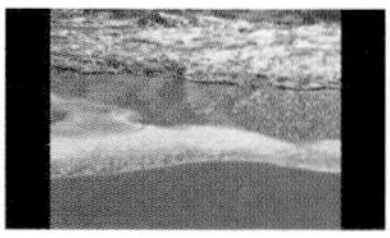

One is Al. Fifty years old. Today he runs a small diner by a motel by the beach. He serves a bustling crowd from behind the lunch counter.

AL: I waited tables in New York for thirty-five years. My wife got sick on me. She wanted to go down to Florida, and here I am.
STANOW: How is business down here in your coffee shop?
AL: It's pretty fair for this type of operation. I mean, you can't get rich, but you work seven days a week and you make a living.
STANOW: What would you say are the conditions of life today for an ordinary working man in America?
AL: Well, I say, for an ordinary man in America he's better off than in any part of Europe or any part of the world. He has more freedom; he has more protection, freedom of speech. At least here, if you don't like the president, you can tell him where to go without being afraid of being put against the wall and shot or being punished. You have freedom of speech.
STANOW: Would you say that this is a land of equal opportunities for all?
AL: It is, if a man has a little ambition. If he's not lazy he can always make a living.

It's not far from the diner to the police station in the middle of town. And it's the same distance from there to a whole other side of America; a different and hotter Hallandale, one that the people on the beach know very little about. However, 20 percent of the town's citizens live there. For

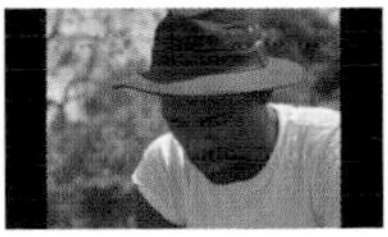

example, John and Roger, twenty-two years old, both as American as the people on the beach.

One-story houses line a sandy road. John and Roger are sitting outside of one, under a palm tree. John wears sunglasses and a tall Afro; Roger wears a white T-shirt, goatee, and broad-brimmed black hat under the beating sun.

STANOW: What was it like coming back to America after having fought over in Vietnam?

JOHN: Almost the same way as before I left, and I say this because, you know, when a man goes to fight for his country and then come back over here and have to almost fight for his life, you know, in certain parts of the country, get ridiculed and discriminated and be less than a man, I don't think is right, you know?

ROGER: Life has its up and downs and hasn't been like I've planned for it to be, you know. Some way I got on the wrong track and I fell into that gutter and I've been trying to get up from there for the longest time. And I think the environment have a whole lot to do with keeping a man down, you know. I've been trying to get out of that gutter for the last four years, but it looks like there's something always holding me down.

Abiodun Oyewole, 2009

Abiodun Oyewole is a writer, teacher, and poet who performs with the spoken-word group The Last Poets.

I mean America is a possibility for everything. America is a young, dumb country, and it needs all kinds of help. America is a dumb puppy with big teeth that bite and hurt. And we take care of America. We hold America in our bosoms, we feed America, we make love to America. There wouldn't be an America if it wasn't for Black people. And so you have some dedicated Black Americans who would die a million deaths to save America. And this is home for us. We don't know really about Africa, we talk about it in a romantic sense, but America's it. And so America's always going to be okay as long as Black people don't totally lose their minds. Because we'll pick up the pieces and we'll turn it into a new dance.

Harlem, 1973

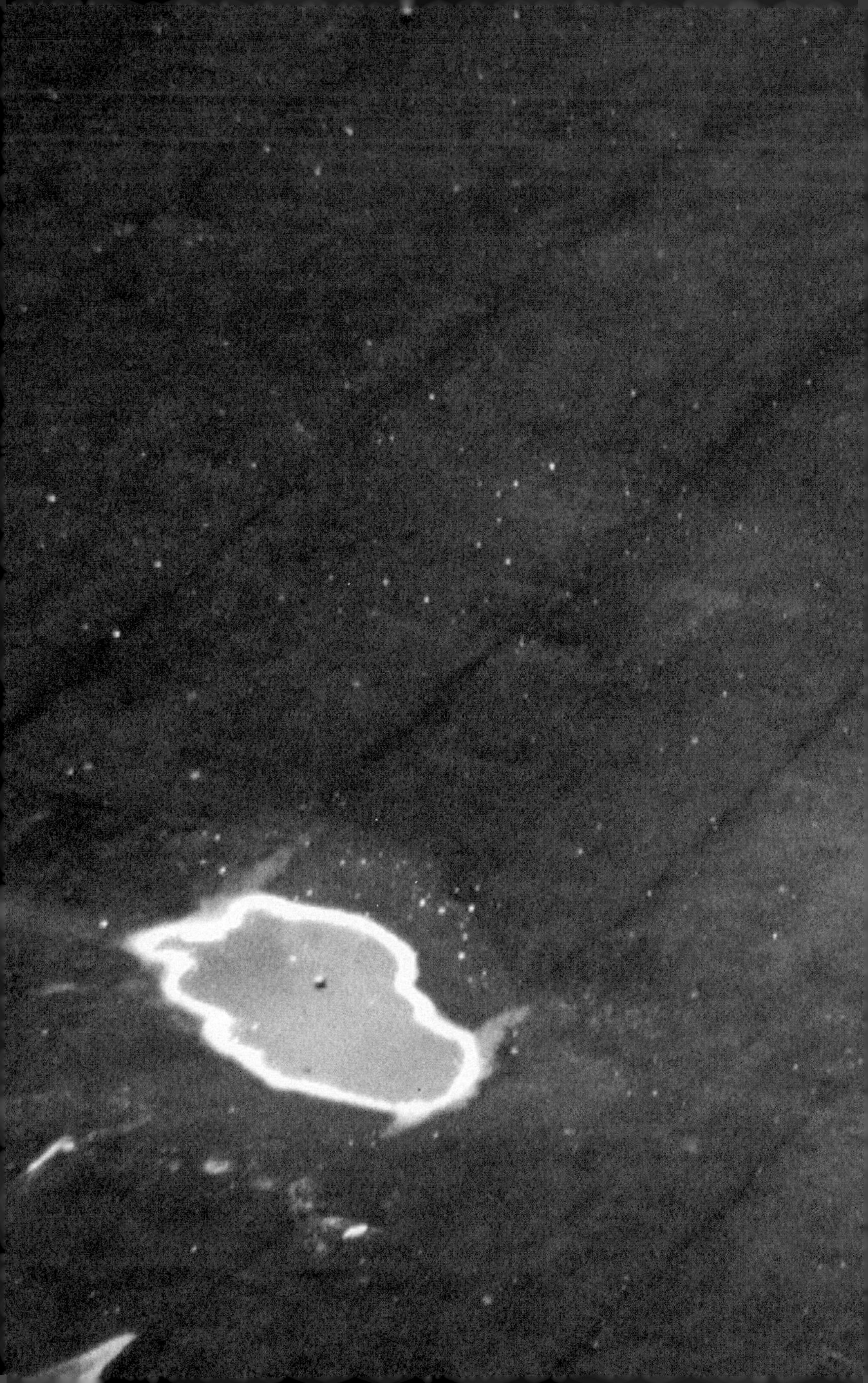

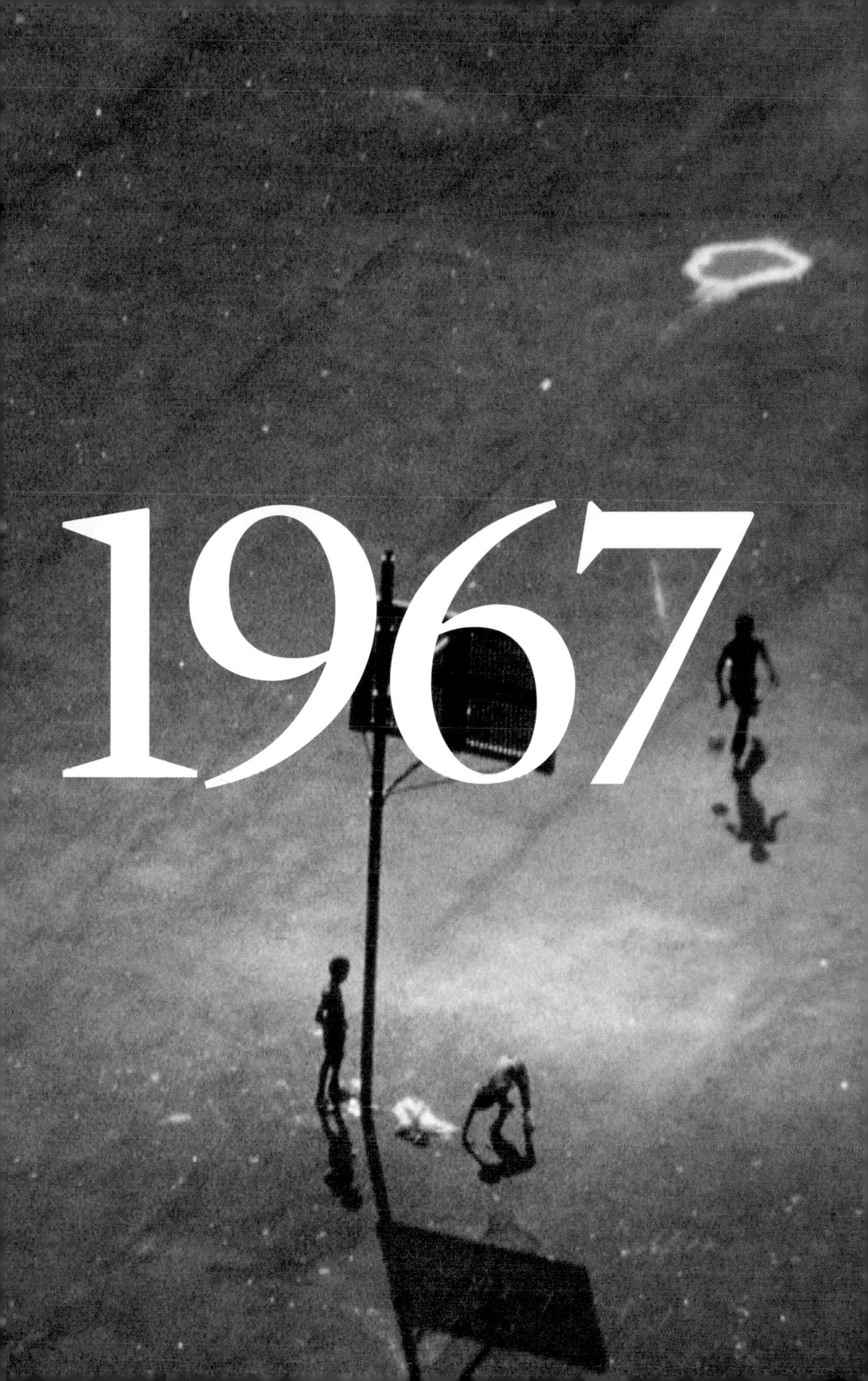
1967

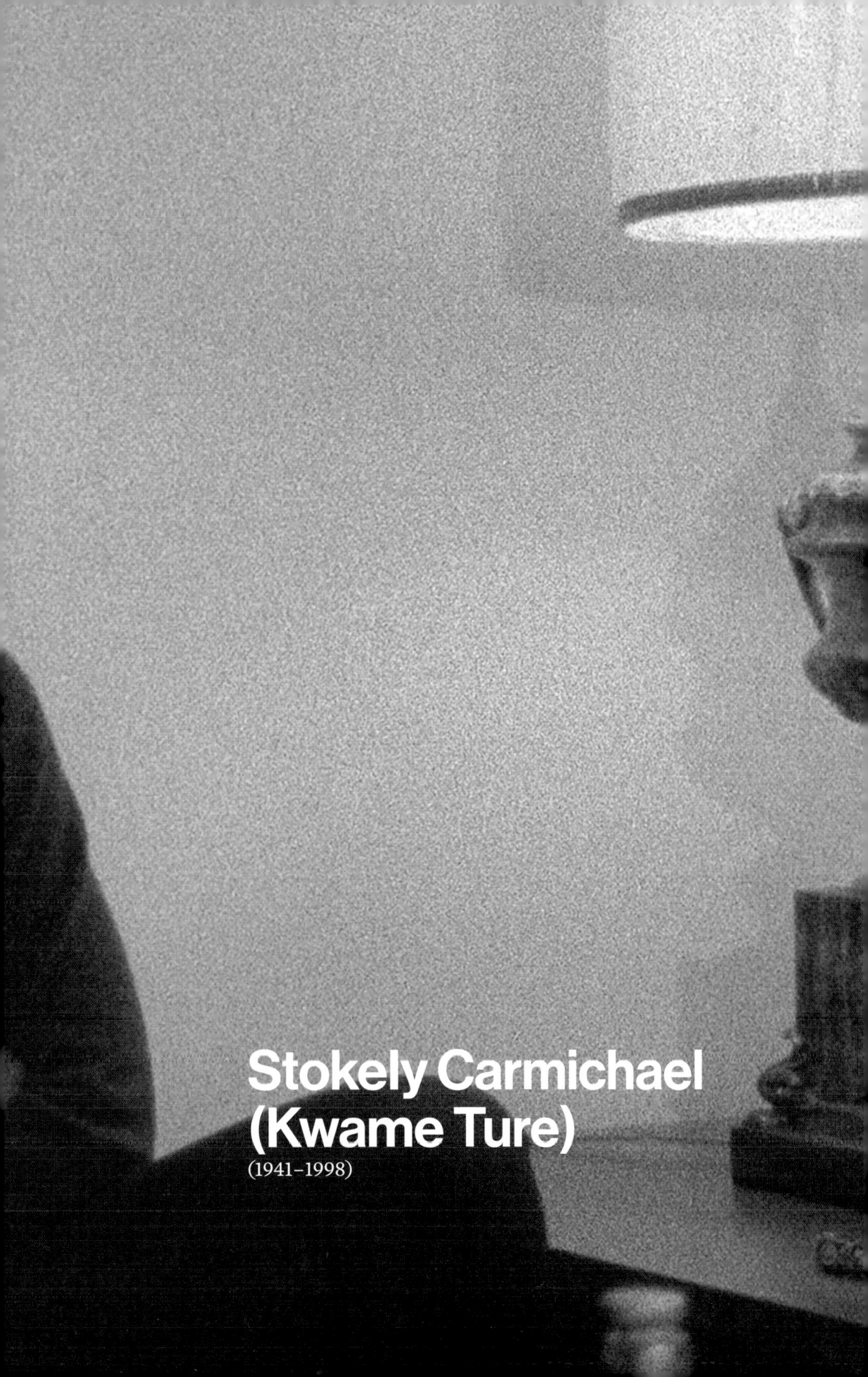

Stokely Carmichael (Kwame Ture)

(1941–1998)

“We been saying ‘Freedom’ for six years. What we are going to start saying now is ‘Black Power!’”

—*Stokely Carmichael*

Black Power!

The revolutionary slogan that raised the fists of a generation was first publicly uttered by Stokely Carmichael.

Stokely Carmichael was eleven when his family immigrated to the Bronx from Trinidad. They were poor; eight family members lived together in a run-down three-room apartment. As a student, Stokely was drawn into the neighborhood's anarchic gang culture, but his entrance into the Bronx High School of Science challenged him in a much more meaningful way and initiated his profoundly fruitful intellectual life. Carmichael began attending Howard University in 1960, the same year that Black students in the South began sitting in at segregated lunch counters, and the bravery of their resistance sparked what would become, in Carmichael, a lifelong fire.

Carmichael spent his freshman year at Howard as a Freedom Rider—participating in a series of bus trips by multiracial groups of activists (known as Freedom Rides) into the South to take part in direct actions that challenged segregation and the Jim Crow system. Like many Freedom Riders, he was arrested many times, and gained the distinction at nineteen of being the youngest member of the Congress of Racial Equality (CORE) to do time: he spent seven weeks in a Mississippi state penitentiary after ignoring a "Whites Only" sign at a train station.

Carmichael joined the Student Nonviolent Coordinating Committee, or SNCC (pronounced "snick"), and threw himself into registering Black voters in the South, at that time a highly charged and dangerous activity. SNCC activists were routinely jailed, beaten, raped, and murdered by segregationists. The civil rights movement, under the leadership of the Reverend Dr. Martin Luther King Jr., was deeply committed to nonviolence even in the face of such horror, but some—Stokely Carmichael among them—were beginning to question whether nonviolent tactics would ever be able to bring about liberation. It was this questioning that led him to cry out for "Black Power"—and marked the genesis of a debate that would shape the political questions of the next decade.

Stockholm, 1967

STOKELY CARMICHAEL: Now let us begin with the modern period of the struggle of Black people in the United States. I guess we could start with 1956, for our generation. This was the beginning of the rise of Dr. Martin Luther King.

Dr. King decided that in Montgomery, Alabama, Black people had to pay the same prices on the buses as did white people, but we had to sit in the back. And we could only sit in the back if every available seat was not taken by a white person. If a white person was standing, a Black person could not sit. So Dr. King and his associates got together and said, "This is inhuman. We will boycott your bus system."

And understand what a boycott is. A boycott is a passive act. It is the most passive political act that anyone can commit, a boycott. Because what the boycott was doing was simply saying: we will not ride your buses. No sort of antagonism. It was not even verbally violent. It was peaceful.

Dr. King's policy was that nonviolence would achieve gains for Black people in the United States. His major assumption was that if you are non-violent, if you suffer, your opponent will see your suffering and will be moved to change his heart. That's very good. He only made one fallacious assumption: in order for nonviolence to work, your opponent must have a conscience. The United States has not, has not, has not.

[The massive crowd applauds.]

Harry Belafonte, 2010

Harry Belafonte is a singer, actor, composer, and activist who has used his fame to promote civil rights and fight for social justice; he is still an activist today.

There's one thing very clever in his argument. He says that the act of not riding on the bus was very passive and that's all it did. He just said "I will not ride on the bus," but he's being very deceitful, what I call intellectually deceitful. Because that was not the objective of the boycott. No boycott, as passive as the act may appear to be, is passive. There's no passivity in a nonviolent movement. What this did was, by stopping the buses from rolling, it seriously affected the economic interests of the community—and once the community began to feel that economic deprivation, the white community got very upset. They thought it was arrogant that the Black people were not appreciative of all that white America had given them, and now they are turning around and biting the hand that fed them. And this idea of boycott is not a passive act—there's nothing passive about nonviolence. I'm passionate about that!

Everything that is done in the civil rights movement is to destabilize the status quo. To destabilize the system so that it has no choice but to negotiate with us on better terms than the ones that we were experiencing. The most difficult thing for Westerners to accept is an act of passivity. It's not in your culture. Western civilization is rooted in anger and in violence and [violence] has always been the tool to settle disagreements.

I admire the concept: it's brilliant, a mixture between Jesus, Gandhi, and King. We don't need anybody to tell us what it is. We know what it is. What bothers me is, why don't we apply it? There exists the great mystery. I admire Stokely.

STOKELY CARMICHAEL: There's a reason why I cannot speak loudly. When I was very small I used to speak very loudly. I used to come home and I yelled, "Hey, mom! I'm home!" And my mother would say, "Black people are not supposed to be loud." 'Cause we were ashamed of being loud, and so I tried to be soft. But I'll try to be loud again.

Harry Belafonte, 2010

A great and powerful woman in our movement, especially in our early years, and also a mentor to Dr. King, was a woman by the name of Ella Baker. She started the Southern Christian Leadership Conference (SCLC) and was in charge of youth affairs. She was that force that attracted and recruited young people to the movement.

That was a very successful recruitment, but as the ranks grew, so did the impatience of the young people. It wasn't so much that they rejected the tenets and the tactics of nonviolence. It was that they did not like the hurdles that were put before them by these old ministers, these older people who came from the life and the tradition that was very different to the energy of the day. They got very frustrated by how long it took to make decisions and they threatened to break away. Ella Baker, knowing that this was coming, suggested to them that they break away—but not without organizing. That they should come together around an independent youth organization, led by them and rooted in the concept of nonviolence. So it was created and it was called the Student Nonviolent Coordinating Committee and all these young students came.

One problem was that they had no money—they had no resources at all. And they came to me, and in the beginning I funded all of the startup mechanisms for the Student Nonviolent Coordinating Committee to become a functioning entity. I reached out not only through my own resources but to others whom I had influence with. So we were able to give SNCC a fairly decent startup purse to get on with the work. SNCC made space for me, they respected me. I could sit in on their most strategic meetings. We could discuss their affairs and they knew they would never be betrayed by me. As a consequence, that endorsement by SNCC and the endorsement by Dr. King and others gave me a powerful position within the struggle to deal directly with negotiations with the White House. So that I had very close contact with, and was passing information, negotiating, and challenging the Justice Department, headed by Bobby Kennedy. And I had a chance to talk with some regularity to John Kennedy on foreign policy and the relationship with the developing world. I was made cultural advisor, answerable directly to the president. It stayed straight ahead until the day they were all assassinated. I watched all my friends get wiped out. One right after the other—and there's more to come.

Stokely Carmichael became chairman of SNCC in 1966. A few weeks after he took office, James Meredith, the civil rights activist who had in 1962 singlehandedly integrated the University of Mississippi, began a solitary "March against Fear" from Memphis, Tennessee, to Jackson, Mississippi, to protest the racist reign of terror that was Jim Crow. Thirty miles into the march, a white man with a shotgun shot Meredith three times, injuring him. In response, Carmichael joined Dr. Martin Luther King Jr. and other activists to continue Meredith's march. They were arrested.

REPORTER: A few words on Martin Luther King?

STOKELY CARMICHAEL: Dr. King is a great man, full of compassion. He is full of mercy and he is very patient. He is a man who could accept the uncivilized behavior of white Americans and their unseasoned taunts and still have in his heart forgiveness.

Unfortunately, I'm from a younger generation and I'm not as patient as Dr. King. Nor am I as merciful as Dr. King. Their unwillingness to deal with someone like Dr. King just means they will have to deal with this younger generation.

Erykah Badu, 2010

Erykah Badu is a Grammy-winning musician, songwriter, and actor.

Stokely was saying that Dr. King was a merciful person, and he was a bit more severe because he was from a younger generation. But mercy without severity is weakness and severity without mercy is cruelty. And those two people were both very necessary because they created a balance that continued to create a perpetuated change.

STOKELY CARMICHAEL: Let us examine the press criticisms. The first one was the outcry of "violence." And the whole world was shocked. How could an African American think of violence? How could we think about violence when all our lives we had been subjugated to violence? We live in the most violent country in the world today. How can we think about violence? It is clear to me that the people who were conjuring up arguments about violence were concerned not about violence but about something else. A different type of violence in the world today. Black violence, Black violence.

Have we not seen white violence? Isn't the United States the most violent country in the world? Does she not bomb Vietnam into oblivion? Does she not invade Cuba? Does she not invade Santo Domingo? Does she not do whatever she pleases whenever she pleases because she has guns to back her up? What then is the shock of violence from within the most violent society? Who is it that has been doing the killing for the United States in all of her dirty wars? Has it not been the Black man? Is it not 45 percent of our brothers today that die in Vietnam?

What is this nonsensical cry about violence? Violence is the highest form of political struggle. When one goes into a political struggle, if one is incapable of solving that political struggle through constitutional means, the logical extension is the gun. That is a law of history. Lenin said that war is the extension of politics. Chairman Mao Tse-tung says that "war is politics with violence, politics is war without violence." Clear? Enough, then, of

Stokely Carmichael with journalists.

Below:
Leaflet for the Swedish SNCC.

this talk of violence. It just is; it just is. The question is: if there is going to be violence, can that violence be used for something good?

Now on the counter side of the question of violence comes the question of peace. The critics then begin to say that "Ah, you are not for peace." You are not for peace, you are violent, you want to create war. I am for peace. Everybody in the world is for peace. Lyndon Johnson is for peace and he's fighting a war in Vietnam for peace. Yes, I am for peace with justice; as long as there is injustice there can be no peace, none whatsoever. None. What. So. Ever.

So that what you have today when people are calling for peace—but they were not really calling for peace, they were calling for a maintenance of the status quo. Law and order, all the time, the first thing they say. We want law and order. Yes, Hitler said the same thing: we want law and order and if the Jews resist, we will kill them. There must be law and order.

I am not concerned with law and order, I am concerned with justice. And what Johnson ought to do every time the rebellious say "let us talk about justice"—because if there is law and order upholding an unjust system, there is always going to be chaos. That is a rule of mankind and it will not be denied in this century. So to those who call for peace, we say to them very, very carefully that to call for peace in the midst of injustice is to be immoral. For where there is injustice there will be no peace, peace, peace.

There comes a time in people's lives when they say "No! Up to this point, enough! But beyond this point, no! You have gone too far."

That's where we are in the United States. You have gone too far. You have raped, you have plundered, you have murdered, you have sent us to war, you continue to exploit. "Enough! No more! From this point on, if you wish to exploit us, you can have it only one way. You will exploit us in our blood if you do not die in the attempt. Period." That is where we are in the United States.

That sounds like violence. I don't think it's violent; I just think it's echoing the words of liberation or death, I think it is just echoing the words of the bravest people in the world today: the Vietnamese. We would rather die than be subjugated to the rule of somebody else, especially the rule of imperialism. So we support the war in Vietnam and we are not like the people who call for peace.

We do not want peace in Vietnam; we want the Vietnamese to defeat the United States of America. That's how you will have peace in that country. That is the only way you will have peace in the country: when the United States is out of Vietnam.

Talib Kweli, 2010

Talib Kweli is a rapper, performer, and activist from Brooklyn, New York. He is also well known for his work in Black Star, his collaboration with Mos Def.

The first thing that crossed my mind with Stokely is he has so much power, passion, and fire inside of him. And he understood what his job was very early on. Even though the things he was saying were in direct opposition to the philosophy of Dr. King, he understood that Dr. King was still important. He understood the compassion.

They studied how to carry it out, they studied the path of resistance. He studied power and what power meant, and if I'm correct, he was the first one to really talk about Black Power and say that in his book. I read that book when I was a teenager, but that's exactly what was missing from the equation—the power—and that was what he was looking for. He was powerful just from the speaking, you know? Stokely Carmichael wasn't even like the Panthers; the Panthers were very influenced by him, but it wasn't like he was in the streets with some guns, you know?

The Bronx, 1967

MABEL CARMICHAEL: Let's see, I think Stokely was a sophomore in college when he went down to Mississippi. And he had called me that evening on the phone and said he's going to Mississippi. I tried to get him, but he wouldn't answer the phone back. And someone told me he had already gone. I knew he was flying, so when that batch got into Mississippi by plane I figured one would be Stokely. I stopped by the phone, by the radio, all day trying to hear what happened. And when I heard they picked up four of them, I knew one of them was Stokely. I think I died a thousand times. It was the first time he'd been to jail.
INGRID DAHLBERG, REPORTER: And all the other times, how did you feel?
MABEL: The same thing. Every time he goes, I die a thousand times.
REPORTER: Oh, really?
STOKELY CARMICHAEL: You want me to do the interview for you?
REPORTER: Would you really? Lovely. *[Stokely joins his mother on the couch as the reporter makes room for him and shows him how to use the microphone. They all laugh.]*

STOKELY: Mrs. Carmichael, when you came to the United States with your children, where did you live?
MABEL: We lived at Stebbins Avenue for a while.
STOKELY: What kind of neighborhood was it?
MABEL: It was kind of a mixed neighborhood, but a little on the run-down side.
STOKELY: What do you mean by "the run-down side"?
MABEL: Streets were dirty, garbage pails all thrown around and not covered and things like that.
STOKELY: How big was the place you lived in?
MABEL: We had a three-room apartment there.
STOKELY: And how many people lived there?
MABEL: When my kids moved to the United States we were still living there, my husband and I, so that made five children—because I had two there, the five that came with their aunt, my husband, and I.
STOKELY: How many is that all together?
MABEL: Five and three, eight.
STOKELY: How many bedrooms?

MABEL: One bedroom.
STOKELY: Where did everybody sleep?
MABEL: Some slept in the living room and the rest of us slept in the bedroom.
STOKELY: Did you think this type of living was conducive to raising a family?
MABEL: No.
STOKELY: How was life in general for your children? I mean, could they do other things most children in the United States could do? And did they have enough money to do those things?
MABEL: No we didn't.
STOKELY: Why didn't they?
MABEL: Because my husband didn't make enough money.
STOKELY: Why didn't he make enough money?
MABEL: He was a carpenter and he worked two weeks in, four weeks off. He would drive a taxicab part of the time.
STOKELY: But there were other carpenters who lived better than your husband?
MABEL: Of course.
STOKELY: And why didn't your husband?
MABEL: Because he was laid off. He was always the first to be laid off.
STOKELY: Why was he always the first to be laid off?
MABEL: Because he was Negro. He always said because he was a colored man, because internally we used the word *colored*, we never used the word *Negro*. So he always said it was because he was a colored man.
STOKELY: Thank you.

Paris, 1967

In 1967, no less than fifty-nine riots (or, depending on your point of view, rebellions) took place in Black communities across the United States—and police blamed Stokely Carmichael's fiery statements for inciting them. Under intense media scrutiny and legal pressure, Carmichael left the United States for a world tour, during which he met with revolutionaries, pan-Africanists, and liberationists in countries including Algeria, Cuba, Puerto Rico, Guinea, Tanzania, Egypt, and North Vietnam. During this trip he became more convinced of pan-Africanist thought, and met the two men after whom he would later rename himself Kwame Ture: Guinean president Sékou Touré and Ghanian leader Kwame Nkrumah. Before his return to the United States, Carmichael gave a press conference to a packed house in Paris.

CARMICHAEL: I don't see myself as a personality—for example, as an entertainer who survives on his own talents. I see myself as more than that, and that strength comes from the base of Black Americans.
REPORTER: But for some people, they might [want to] see you dead.
CARMICHAEL: Oh, I'm afraid that you'll always find people like that, but I don't think it's my job to be concerned with that. For example, I don't think that if I die tomorrow—which is a possibility—that what I've said will just die. I don't think so.
REPORTER: Are you afraid to be killed?
CARMICHAEL: Yes, I'm afraid to be killed.
REPORTER: By whom?
CARMICHAEL: By anyone, the CIA or some lunatic. But I don't think we can let fear immobilize us. I think we have to do whatever we have to do and be willing to accept the consequences.
REPORTER: Are you going to return to the United States?
CARMICHAEL: I most certainly am. There's 50 million Blacks who are living in the United States and those Africans have to be organized to fight for their liberation.
REPORTER: Isn't there a possibility that you might end up in jail on your arrival?
CARMICHAEL: I was born in jail. [Applause.] They're getting scared now 'cause Black people are organizing and they're putting people in jail and they're losing their cool.
REPORTER: Nevertheless, we heard you didn't have enough money for your airfare out of this country. How are you going? Where is the money going to come from during your stay in this country?
CARMICHAEL: My fairy godmother.

Stokely Carmichael with his mother, Mabel Carmichael, at her home in the Bronx, 1967.

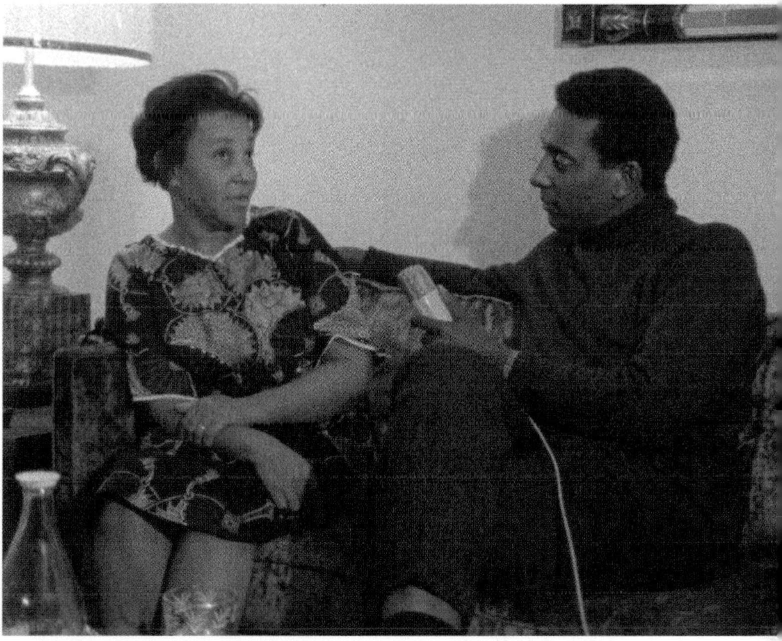

STOKELY CARMICHAEL, SINGING:
No way to turn.
Burn, baby, burn.
Called President Johnson on the telephone,
Humphrey said he wasn't at home.
Tried to get hold of Dr. Martin Luther King,
But Abernathy said he wasn't there,
Couldn't get no oil from the Rockefeller well,
I couldn't get no diamonds from his mines. Yeah, yeah.
If I can't enjoy the American dream,
It won't be water, but the fire next time.
So I say burn, baby, burn.
Burn, baby, burn.

SPEAKING: This is for the FBI. Nothing is wasted. Everything just takes a different form. What form will you take?

Talib Kweli, 2010

A few years ago, I was listening to Stokely Carmichael speeches while I was preparing for a new record I was working on. It was shortly after 9/11 in America, it was maybe 2003, 2002, and while I was listening to his speech I was on hold on the telephone, making a reservation on JetBlue Airlines to fly to California.

When I got to the airport the FBI, the CIA, the TSA, they came and intercepted me. All these guys in black suits took me into a back room and started questioning me about the Stokely Carmichael speech I was listening to. What they told me was that the airline, the person I spoke to when I was making the reservation, heard the speech in the background and called them, but they probably had some sort of bug or some sort of tap or something. But they were very concerned with me listening to the Stokely Carmichael speech from 1967, forty years ago.

So these words that he said still are a threat. We have gangster rappers who talk about shooting and killing other people all the time, but the FBI is not looking for them—they're looking at me, because I'm listening to his speech forty years ago. It shows you the power of those words, that they resonate even now. The FBI is still scared of this man. He changed his name to Kwame Ture, they put him in jail a bunch of

Stokely Carmichael burning letters in Paris.

Below:
Stokely Carmichael arriving at Detroit Airport.

times. He doesn't have nearly the same influence over our community as he did then, but yet they still stop me at the airport for listening to his speech.

Another thing I noticed was, when you see images of Stokely, you only see the speeches. This is the first time I've seen something where he is just hanging out, with white people, hanging out with his mother, and he just seems like a regular dude. And that is what you don't realize about these people: none of these people are evil or bad or even extra violent, it's just, to them common sense meant that they had to speak and stand up for themselves. So all you see is this image of them standing up for themselves so it makes you think that they are like that all the time, but he just was a regular dude—and that was what I got from that footage with his mom.

Sonia Sanchez, 2010

Sonia Sanchez is a renowned author, poet, playwright, and scholar from Philadelphia.

As I listen to Stokely, or Kwame Ture, as he became later, I just remember the fire and the ideas that he talked about. We in the North, radical Blacks in the North, we were called Malcolm's children. Because Malcolm was here in the North and we listened a lot to what he had to say. And we were not really Martin's children, if you understand that. But we appreciated our dear brother Martin and we understood the need that his movement was all about in the South, in terms of desegregating. So he was very important to us.

Martin Luther King Jr., New York City, April 4, 1967

As I have walked among the desperate, rejected, and angry young men, I have told them that Molotov cocktails and rifles would not solve their problems. I have tried to offer them my deepest compassion while maintaining my conviction that social change comes most meaningfully through nonviolent action; for they ask and write me, "So what about Vietnam?" They ask if our nation wasn't using massive doses of violence to solve its problems to bring about the changes it wanted. Their questions hit home, and I knew that I could never again raise my voice against the violence of the oppressed in the ghettos without first having spoken clearly to the greatest purveyor of violence in the world today: my own government. For the sake of those boys, for the sake of this government, for the sake of the hundreds of thousands trembling under our violence, I cannot be silent.

1968

Dr. Martin Luther King and Harry Belafonte

“I could never again raise my voice against the violence of the oppressed in the ghettos without first having spoken clearly to the greatest purveyor of violence in the world today: my own government.”

—*Martin Luther King Jr.*

Nineteen Sixty-Eight

Questlove, 2010

Ahmir-Khalib "Questlove" Thompson is a musician, journalist, and record producer best known for his work in the hip-hop group the Roots.

You're really naive if you truly think that Martin Luther King just happened to be at the wrong place at the wrong time at the Lorraine Motel and this random guy just came and shot and killed him. Oh, no. Martin Luther King sort of had a change of heart; Martin Luther King was starting to take a more militant, stronger position. And his new battle was no war. Government was like, whoa, wait, he is about to come into our territory. Like it's one thing to let you take a shit in the same toilet that I do—I'll give you that—but you ain't about to stop my money flow. Huh-uh. You got to go.

Angela Davis, 2010

Angela Davis, whose important work on behalf of the Black Power movement is featured throughout this book, is today retired from her professorship in the History of Consciousness program at the University of California, Santa Cruz.

It's very important to point out that Dr. Martin Luther King was the first prominent public figure to speak out against the war in Vietnam. And there were those on both sides who felt that it wasn't his role to take a position on Vietnam. There were, of course, those in the government that said that you are a civil rights leader, you have nothing to do with the war. And then there were those in the movement who were saying, we're struggling for freedom for Black people. This has nothing to do with the war in Vietnam. But of course it had an enormous amount to do with the war in Vietnam. And eventually, especially after Dr. King made his powerful speech in the Riverside Church in which he talked about the connection between militarism and racism, we recognized that there was no way to imagine justice and equality inside the country as long as racism was being used as a weapon to attack the people of Vietnam.

And so, for some of us throughout that period, we always linked the two struggles. The struggle at home, the struggle abroad; struggles against racism; struggles for peace; struggles for what during World War II many activists, and especially communist activists, talked about as the "double V"—the victory against fascism abroad and victory against racism at home. And we also said the victory of the people of Vietnam would advance the struggles of people of color inside the country, the issues of racism and the issues of sexism and working-class people's rights, et cetera. And I think that, thanks to Black feminists especially, this notion of intersectionality, of being able to address multiple issues simultaneously, was quite powerful.

Harry Belafonte, 2010

HARRY BELAFONTE: There was a very popular show here in the US called the *Johnny Carson Show*. It's a night talk show, and I hosted that show for a week. And in that week I had Bobby Kennedy and Dr. King and a bunch of high-profile citizens from around the world who the American public do not get a chance to hear much about or to know much about their personal lives. So that week I had as many as I could get to be part of the panels and the discussion. The night that Dr. King was on, when we spoke about death, I asked him if he feared for his life. And he said, not really—he'd overcome his fear of death and his preoccupation with it and was now focused not on how long he would live, but on what would be the quality of the time that he would live. So he was more focused on how much good he was doing, not focused on how long he would be here.

And from the very beginning, when he was stabbed in Harlem and the knife blade was just a precarious few millimeters from his heart, and then if anybody tried to move it or, the doctor said, if Dr. King had sneezed, he would have been dead—from those days, which were the earliest in his life as a movement leader. And then later on, his home was bombed and so many attempts to harm him and to murder him. Eventually we knew that he would—there was the great possibility that he would—pay the supreme price and that someone would murder him. So when it happened, it was a great sense of sadness and we were all emotionally overwhelmed with the loss. But I think many of us—not all of us—expected that in this America, that this would probably be the way in which he would leave us, and it was a rather pathetic thought because it was exactly what happened. There was a sadness, there was a huge sense of loss.

GÖRAN HUGO OLSSON: Do you remember where you were when it happened?

BELAFONTE: Yes, I was in my home in New York. He had just left us a couple of nights before, because we held a strategy planning in my home, as we did when we began to launch major phases of where the movement would go and what new goals we had set for ourselves. Our agenda was vast—and then he came to the final moment in our agenda where we said that it's no longer about race, it's now about the welfare and the well-being of human life. We must talk about economics; we must talk about why people are poor. We must galvanize our nation to begin to take care of the poor. America should not have poor people. No one should ever go to bed hungry, there should be gainful employment, there should be a living wage, there should be access to health care with no charge. We should have education for free, like so many nations successfully have applied and have benefited from.

All these things put a huge bull's-eye on Dr. King, because he was now tampering with the playground of the wealthy. He was now tampering with America's main nerve, main artery, in the interest of the powerful. And when he came to that moment of dismantling the economic construct, he had to go. Many of us anticipated it, but of course our deepest hope was that we would be wrong, that we would have a service and that he would pass away from natural causes, but that was not the case.

Martin Luther King Jr., Memphis, 1968

The night before his assassination, Martin Luther King Jr. spoke in support of striking Memphis sanitation workers, a speech that captured some of the more radical shifts in his politics as well as acknowledging the imminence of his own death.

Now we're going to march again, and we've got to march again, in order to put the issue where it is supposed to be—and force everybody to see that there are thirteen hundred of God's children here suffering, sometimes going hungry, going through dark and dreary nights wondering how this thing is going to come out. That's the issue. And we've got to say to the nation: We know how it's coming out. For when people get caught up with that which is right and they are willing to sacrifice for it, there is no stopping point short of victory.

We aren't going to let any mace stop us. We are masters in our nonviolent movement in disarming police forces; they don't know what to do. I've seen them so often. I remember in Birmingham, Alabama, when we were in that majestic struggle there, we would move out of the Sixteenth Street Baptist Church day after day; by the hundreds we would move out. And Bull Connor would tell them to send the dogs forth, and they did come; but we just went before the dogs singing, "Ain't gonna let nobody turn me around." . . . Well, I don't know what will happen now. We've got some difficult days ahead. But it really doesn't matter with me now, because I've been to the mountaintop.

And I don't mind.

Like anybody, I would like to live a long life. Longevity has its place. But I'm not concerned about that now. I just want to do God's will. And He's allowed me to go up to the mountain. And I've looked over. And I've seen the Promised Land. I may not get there with you. But I want you to know tonight, that we, as a people, will get to the Promised Land!

Kathleen Cleaver, 2010

Kathleen Neal Cleaver was the national communication secretary of the Black Panther Party from 1967 to 1971. After 1971 she lived in exile in Mexico, Algeria, and Cuba with her then-husband, the Panther leader Eldridge Cleaver, after he was wounded in a police shootout and fled the country. Kathleen Cleaver later went on to study law at Yale and is now a professor at the school of law at Emory University.

On April 4, 1967, in Riverside Church, Martin Luther King publicly condemned the Vietnam War and asked how he could counsel young men to remain peaceful when "the government of the US is the greatest purveyor of violence in the world."

So he had moved from being a spokesperson and leader in civil rights to a person condemning, essentially, foreign policy. On April 4, 1968, he was shot through the head.

And then Bobby Kennedy, who was going to be an incredible candidate for the Democratic nomination for president, was killed.

And in the following year, in December, the Black Panther leader Fred Hampton, the most eloquent and charismatic and effective spokesperson in the Black Panther Party at that time, he was twenty-one years old when he was murdered in what—you can only can call it a conspiracy. An FBI and police conspiracy that went up to the highest levels.

So then, you see, there is a systematic decision to prevent the radical leaders from having their natural effect. I mean it's always difficult to mobilize people, but when in a short time if you eliminate Martin Luther King, Robert Kennedy, Fred Hampton, not to mention all the others who were being killed, you diminish the strength of that movement. And so had King chosen to be more cowardly, maybe he would have lived longer, but that's not the choice he made.

Of course if Fred Hampton, who had tremendous leadership potential, had remained alive and had to exercise the abilities and talents as a leader in organizing, things would be different. I mean, he was phenomenal and built the biggest and the strongest organization, and also the coalition called the Rainbow Coalition with the Young Lords and the Young Patriots and Black Panthers, and also worked with gangs. He attracted everyone. Suppose Fred Hampton and Martin Luther King and Malcolm X and Robert Kennedy and John Kennedy had all lived. So it's not just one, it's a cluster of ideas and support that was annihilated.

Above:
King Gustav VI Adolf of Sweden, Dr. King, Harry Belafonte, Coretta Scott King, and Gunnar Myrdal.

Right:
Kid challenging the police in Brooklyn, 1968.

Erykah Badu, 2010

I have no idea. I don't know if Dr. King was changing his mind. I don't know that. Everything I saw from him was deliberate, you know. His thinking was a product of his upbringing, what he believed. He was born and genetically generated to do the things that he did. There's a thing inside of him that made him who he is. He was a totally necessary component in our evolution and our evolving as people. I salute Dr. King, I salute Stokely Carmichael, I salute all of those who have come before us. Who have unselfishly given their time and their private lives and their family time and risked their lives. To push us as people to another place, to wake us out of our complacency. I think it's important, I think it's necessary, I think it's what they were born to do. Reverend Dr. Martin Luther King Jr. was born to say those things that he said. I have no critique or no opinion.

Abiodun Oyewole, 2010

In 1968 Martin Luther King was killed, Robert Kennedy was killed, Medgar Evers was killed, Mark Clark and Fred Hampton were killed, Tommie Smith and John Carlos did the Black Power salute in Mexico City. I mean it's a litany of things that took place in '68, like that was the moving stone from in front of the cave in '68. I mean it really was a special beginning and opening, and unfortunately, any time we have raised a thing as an opening, death accompanies those things.

Stokely Carmichael, April 5, 1968

White America killed Dr. King. They had absolutely no reason to do so. He was the one man in our race who was trying to teach our people to have love, compassion, and mercy for what white people had done. When white America killed Dr. King, she declared war on us. The rebellions that have been occurring around the cities of this country is just light stuff to what is about to happen. We have to retaliate for the death of our leaders. The execution of those deaths will not be in the courtrooms, they are going to be in the streets of the United States of America.

Abiodun Oyewole, 2010

There were many sacrifices. When they say "we stand on the shoulders of people," we are actually in the palms of the hands of a lot of folks, because we were moved and motivated and charged up by people who had already made a commitment in the sixties to bring about change. And even though I was really on the periphery—I was on the outside looking in, I didn't know much—I knew I wanted to be a part of the Black Power movement, but I didn't know how to be a part of it. But I felt it was something necessary. Now what he did—I still could not have marched with Dr. King—I could never have been with him on any level. I did not agree with his philosophy and I still don't agree with his philosophy. I do agree with fighting fire with fire—I'm not going to fight fire with water, necessarily. And if someone charges at me, I'm going to defend myself. Dr. King was not about that, but what he did do, exposing the demons that existed in America, that's priceless. I mean, it was a sacrifice, but he showed you: This is America, look at this. I mean we're nonviolent, we're singing "we shall overcome" and they got the dogs on us, they're putting us in prison, they're beating the hell out of us. And of course when he was killed I was shattered, just by the fact that this man wasn't fighting with the guns and the weapons that they are fighting with, so I personally felt an insult to that. But I could have never marched. Malcolm's concepts and theories about how we should deal with ourselves and how we should function in this society, that's what made sense to me, so when you look at the Last Poets you're really looking at the disciples of Malcolm X.

Malcolm X, Oxford, England, 1964

As long as a white man does it, it's all right. A Black man is supposed to have no feelings. But when a Black man strikes back, he's an extremist. He's supposed to sit passively and have no feelings, be nonviolent and love his enemy, no matter what kind of attack—be it verbal or otherwise—he's supposed to take it, but if he stands up and in any way tries to defend himself, then he is an extremist.

Robert F. Kennedy follows the hearse at Dr. King's funeral, 1968.

Below:
Riots after Dr. King's assassination.

New York, 1968

A young Black boy in a track jacket speaks to reporter Bertil Askelöf of Swedish Television.

BOY: Well, the unrest that is now in Harlem is kind of just starting and I think it's going to grow and grow much larger. And it isn't entirely the Harlemers' fault, because most of the people in Harlem are Negroes and it seems as though most of the big stores or anything that really makes money is owned by a person of another race. And they're kind of kept down from achieving any kind of goals for themselves. You could say the three heroes of this century have been just cut down in the prime of youth.

REPORTER: Which heroes are you thinking of?

BOY: John Fitzgerald Kennedy, Martin Luther King Jr., and Robert Francis Kennedy.

VOICEOVER: The assassination of Robert Kennedy has shaken the USA. This is outside St. Patrick's Cathedral in New York, where Robert Kennedy is lying in state. Many fear that the US was too late in introducing social reforms that could have provided over 30 million poor in the slums with a more humane existence. And too late to stem the rising tide of alarm in the Negro community and avoid new conflicts and further political assassinations.

YOUNG MAN: There ain't no future, that's all there is to it. No future at all.

REPORTER: Why don't you think there's a future?

YOUNG MAN: Kennedy gets killed, they killed King, they killed Evers, they're killing all the people that do something for the Black man, that stood up for him. Those are the only men who really stood up for him. And I don't know, it seems like there is a conspiracy. People say maybe there isn't. But I think it really is. It has to be something.

YOUNG WOMAN: I don't think there is much of a future at this point.

REPORTER: You mean for Black people?

YOUNG WOMAN: Not much future at all, they're just killing everybody.

REPORTER: For the nation?

YOUNG WOMAN: For the nation itself. For the nation itself.

BO HOLMSTRÖM, REPORTER: It's 7 a.m. in the dark, worn-out rooms on Hopkinson Avenue. Margie Mayle dresses her ten kids. Two have a cold, one can't find his shoes. All are sleepy, all are hungry. It's a day like all the others. To Margie Mayle, everything is as it ever was. The older children don't even get any breakfast. The small children get what's left in the house. This morning it's only cornflakes, without milk.

Yesterday, on the old television set, President Nixon was flickering. The true facts are, he said, that a huge part of us do not get enough food in order to stay healthy. He promised a strong offensive against hunger in America. But he did not mention that 25 to 30 million people in America go hungry.

But Margie Mayle knows that already. She also knows that in a new book, *Let Them Eat Promises: The Politics of Hunger*, author Nick Kotz accuses President Nixon of instructing the administration: "Use all the rhetoric you want on hunger, as long as it doesn't cost money." Now it's not fair to say only that, because recently President Nixon called a big summit on hunger, with three thousand participants. After three days, the summit demanded free meals in schools, extended programs for food coupons, and a national minimum income.

MARGIE MAYLE: There's no milk to put in it now. Yeah, come on now, baby, eat some of that, then. Eat it, it tastes like cookies, taste it.

Erykah Badu, 2010

I see it all over the world. The same thing, you know. There's more than enough for everyone. But I think that some of our leaders encourage selfishness in the idea of fear and consumption. Being afraid that you won't have enough also perpetuates greed. It reminds me of when I was in elementary school. We learned all of the American songs and one in particular.

Can I sing it? It says:

I want a world where kids can play, and plenty of food to eat.
I want a world where I can speak, and know that I'll be free.
I want a world where kids can talk, and God's above and something . . .
I want a world just like America, like the USA.
Because even though perfect it's not, it's the best thing this world's got.

Those types of songs taught us not to question our government, and to be grateful for everything we got and what was going on. But we

The home of Margie Mayle, Hopkinson Avenue, Brooklyn, New York.

Below: Dr. King addresses Memphis sanitation workers the night before his assassination.

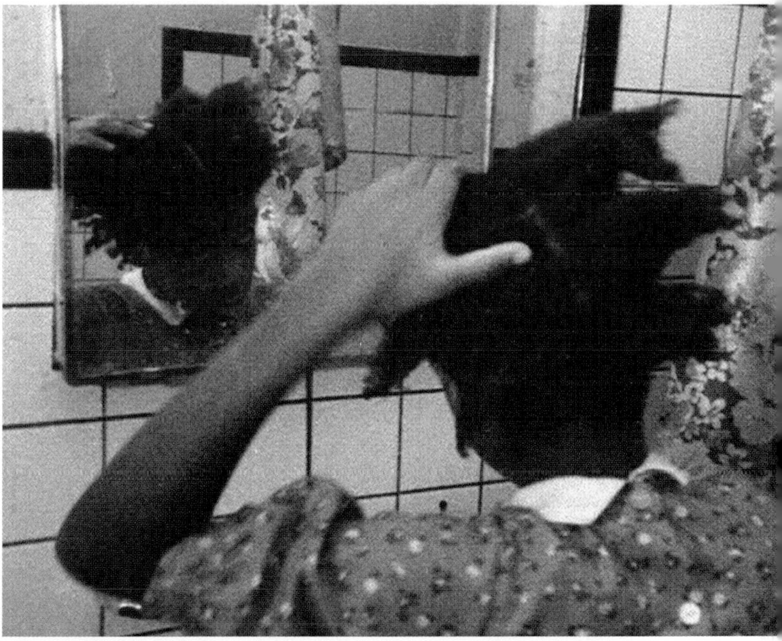

New York City, 1968.

didn't know that it was at the expense of many other people in our own country and all over the world. Because you were taught to fear that you don't have enough and want and want and want. So it perpetuates greed. We are punished for what we are taught. We're kept uneducated, sick, and depressed. We get addicted to something. Now we are under arrest, and it's as sick to us as a game is being played, and it's okay, though, because we will eventually wake up.

There's a happy ending, but with unhappy mistakes first. And one of the biggest mistakes is the greed.

San Francisco, 1968

STOKELY CARMICHAEL: *The birth of this nation was conceived in the genocide of the red man.*
Genocide of the red man.
Of the red man.

Sonia Sanchez, 2010

I was in San Francisco helping to begin Black Studies when Stokely came with his cadre to San Francisco to merge with the Black Panther Party. And I remember the gorgeous signs that they made. I remember the meeting, the big evening at the Fillmore Auditorium. And what we began to see at that point was the fusion of the Southern movement with the Northern movement to form quite a group of young people who were looking at the world in a way that did not necessarily say nonviolence, but it didn't say violence. It merely said, at some point, let's take the movement a step further.

COINTELPRO

The government in all the years of the civil rights movement, while making concessions through Congress, was acting through the FBI to harass and break up black militant groups. Between 1956 and 1971 the FBI concluded a massive Counterintelligence Program (COINTELPRO) that took 295 actions against black groups. Black militancy seemed stubbornly resistant to destruction.

—Howard Zinn, *A People's History of the United States*

The purpose of this new counterintelligence endeavor is to expose, disrupt, misdirect, discredit, or otherwise neutralize the activities of black nationalist, hate-type organizations and groupings, their leadership, spokesmen, membership, and supporters, and to counter their propensity for violence and civil disorder. . . . Particular emphasis should be given to extremists who direct the activities and policies of revolutionary or militant groups such as Stokely Carmichael.

—Internal memo from FBI director J. Edgar Hoover, August 25, 1967

Black leaders, and Stokely Carmichael in particular, were the targets of smears, blackmail attempts, and other intimidation tactics by the federal government as part of the anti–New Left COINTELPRO initiative. One tactic was "pretext" telephone calls, in which the caller pretended to be someone he wasn't. Mabel Carmichael, Stokely's mother, received such a call warning that the Panthers were going to assassinate her son. Stokely Carmichael fled New York the following day and flew to Africa, where he remained in exile for the rest of his life, taking the name Kwame Ture and devoting his life to studying and writing in Guinea.

Eldridge Cleaver, San Francisco, 1968

Eldridge Cleaver, the Black Panther Party's minister of information, would flee the country the following year to escape charges after a police shootout.

I believe that a time has come, a point has been reached, where a line has to be drawn. There's a favorite line: there is a point where caution ends and cowardice begins.

Oakland, California, 1971.

All three of these pigs that we have a choice of, *oink* Nixon, *oink* Humphrey, and *oink* Wallace—they're not for us. They do not represent the best interest of this country. They definitely don't represent the best thinking in this country. In fact they represent the very worst tradition which was ever to crawl from beneath the rocks in this bankrupt country.

Erykah Badu, 2010

It's almost like being asked: Do you believe in violence or not? No, it's awful, it's a bad thing, it's wrong to punish people because of how they look or their culture or their kind. That's wrong, it's always been wrong.

It's right to defend yourself against anything or anyone. And if any country says it's wrong, they're wrong. It's almost like: do as I say, not as I do. You know, it's like punishing a child for doing what he sees the mother do, it's wrong, it's absolutely wrong.

No, we don't believe in violence. We don't believe in killing. We don't believe in harming or hurting. We weren't the ones who inflicted pain and harm on people. We weren't the ones who kidnapped a whole culture of people and brought them to do service for us. We didn't do that, we don't want that, we didn't ask for that. It's wrong, it's not right; it's not a part of the laws of love and giving. And because of that we stand and fight back and want peace. We want to work with pride. Love and live and grow with pride, that's what we want. That's all we want. And to say that we're wrong to defend ourselves is idiotic. Seriously twisted. Shame on America for that; shame on any person who judges someone for defending himself or his family. Shame.

1969

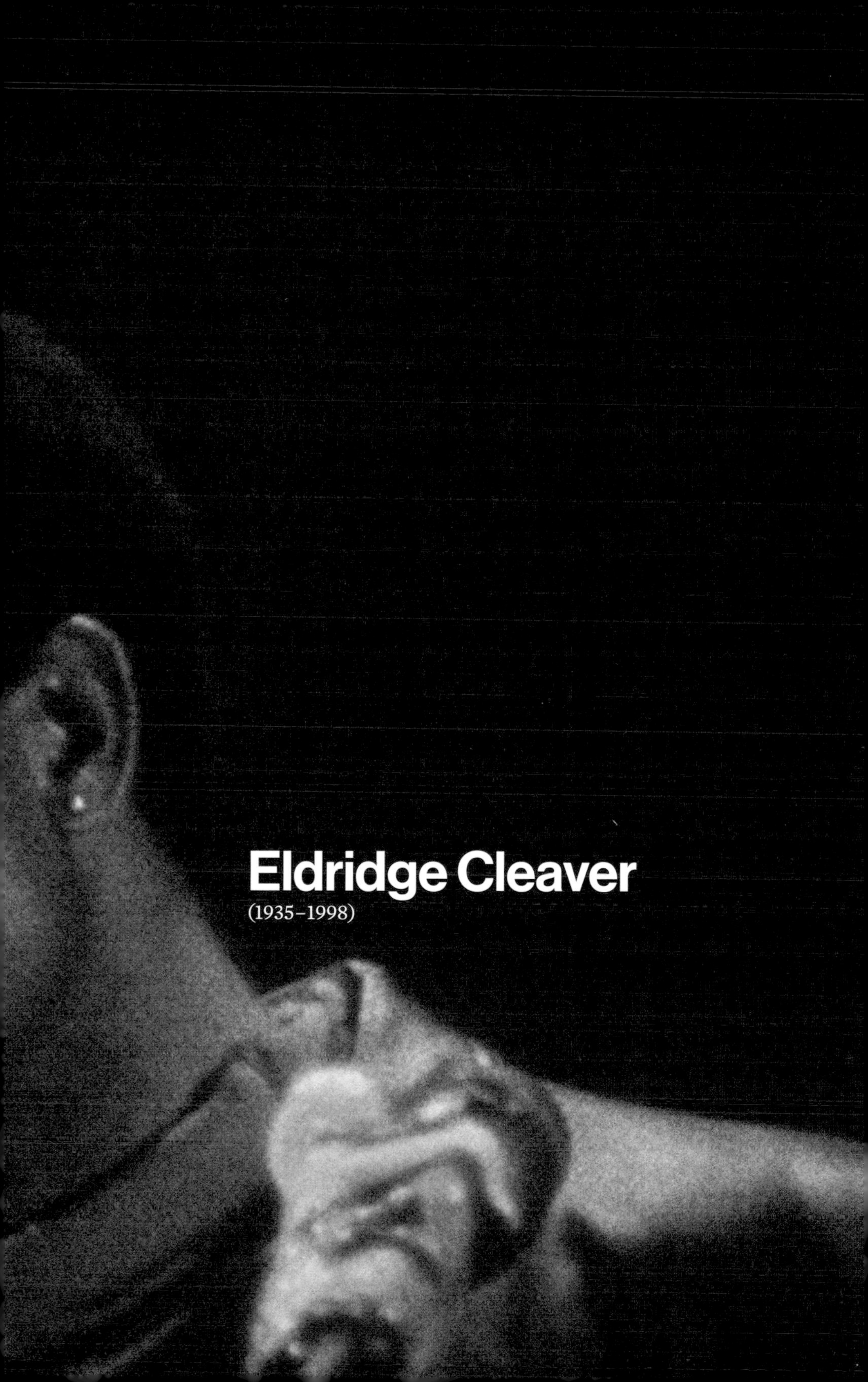

Eldridge Cleaver

(1935–1998)

“We will protect ourselves from the force and violence of the racist police and the racist military, by whatever means necessary.”

—Black Panther Party Ten-Point Program

Black Panther Party Headquarters, Oakland, California, 1969

KIDS SINGING:
Well I got a solution for the revolution, —oh yeah
People gonna see how it feels to be free, —oh yeah
'Cause we sick of pigs lying —oh yeah
And we sick of brothers dying —oh yeah
So come on people, join in the struggle —oh yeah
Fight for liberation —oh yeah
For each and every generation. —oh yeah
I said gun, pick up the gun,
pick up the gun and put the pigs on the run,
pick up the gun.
One more time—
Gun, pick up the gun,
pick up the gun and put the pigs on the run, pick up the gun.

ÖRJAN ÖBERG, REPORTER: This is the Black Panthers' central headquarters. From here, the Party's forty-four divisions and its embassy in Algiers are run. From here, the FNL [Front de Liberation Nationale, the revolutionary anticolonial party in Algeria] has offered Black troops to fight the USA in Vietnam. From here they arrange a series of social activities for the poor in the ghettos.

The headquarters has several times been in firefights with the police—the "pigs," as the Panthers call them. Because of that, the Panthers are utterly suspicious of strangers. The Black Panthers have existed for about four years. They are the most militant Black organization in the USA.

Not only do the Black Panthers offer free breakfast and lunch programs to help the poor to deal with the police, landlords, and authorities, they also offer free clothes and legal defense to political prisoners. Party members receive medical and weapons training.

KIDS SINGING:
All power to the people. All power to the people.
Free Bobby. Free Bobby.
Free Ericka. Free Ericka.
Free Angela. Free Angela.
Free all political prisoners. Free all political prisoners.
Right on. Right on.

The Black Panther Party Ten-Point Program

In 1966 the Black Panther Party published its manifesto and by 1969 the Ten-Point Program was known around the world. Its inclusion of two paragraphs from the Declaration of Independence underscored the parallel between the American Revolution and the Panthers' revolutionary struggle.

1. *We want freedom. We want power to determine the destiny of our Black community.* We believe that Black people will not be free until we are able to determine our destiny.

2. *We want full employment for our people.* We believe that the federal government is responsible and obligated to give every man employment or a guaranteed income. We believe that if the white American businessmen will not give full employment, then the means of production should be taken from the businessmen and placed in the community so that the people of the community can organize and employ all of its people and give a high standard of living.

3. *We want an end to the robbery by the white man of our Black Community.* We believe this racist government has robbed us, and now we are demanding the overdue debt of forty acres and two mules. Forty acres and two mules were promised 100 years ago as restitution for slave labor and mass murder of Black people. We will accept the payment as currency which will be distributed to our many communities. The Germans are now aiding the Jews in Israel for the genocide of the Jewish people. The Germans murdered six million Jews. The American racist has taken part in the

slaughter of over twenty million Black people; therefore, we feel that this is a modest demand that we make.

4. *We want decent housing, fit for shelter of human beings.* We believe that if the white landlords will not give decent housing to our Black community, then the housing and the land should be made into cooperatives so that our community, with government aid, can build and make decent housing for its people.

5. *We want education for our people that exposes the true nature of this decadent American society. We want education that teaches us our true history and our role in the present-day society.* We believe in an educational system that will give to our people a knowledge of self. If a man does not have knowledge of himself and his position in society and the world, then he has little chance to relate to anything else.

6. *We want all Black men to be exempt from military service.* We believe that Black people should not be forced to fight in the military service to defend a racist government that does not protect us. We will not fight and kill other people of color in the world who, like Black people, are being victimized by the white racist government of America. We will protect ourselves from the force and violence of the racist police and the racist military, by whatever means necessary.

7. *We want an immediate end to police brutality and murder of Black people.* We believe we can end police brutality in our Black community by organizing Black self-defense groups that are dedicated to defending our Black community from racist police oppression and brutality. The Second Amendment to the Constitution of the United States gives a right to bear arms. We therefore believe that all Black people should arm themselves for self-defense.

8. *We want freedom for all Black men held in federal, state, county and city prisons and jails.* We believe that all Black people should be released from the many jails and prisons because they have not received a fair and impartial trial.

9. *We want all Black people when brought to trial to be tried in court by a jury of their peer group or people from their Black communities, as defined by the Constitution of the United States.* We believe that the courts should follow the United States Constitution so that Black people will receive fair trials. The Fourteenth Amendment of the U.S. Constitution gives a man a right to be tried by his peer group. A peer is a person from a similar economic,

Woman serving free breakfast, Oakland, 1971.

Below:
Police car outside Black Panther Party Headquarters.

The Black Panther Party's Free Breakfast Program, 1971.

Below:
Black Panther Party Meeting, Oakland, 1971.

social, religious, geographical, environmental, historical and racial background. To do this the court will be forced to select a jury from the Black community from which the Black defendant came. We have been, and are being, tried by all-white juries that have no understanding of the "average reasoning man" of the Black community.

10. *We want land, bread, housing, education, clothing, justice and peace. And as our major political objective, a United Nations–supervised plebiscite to be held throughout the Black colony in which only Black colonial subjects will be allowed to participate for the purpose of determining the will of Black people as to their national destiny.*

When in the Course of human events, it becomes necessary for one people to dissolve the political bands which have connected them with another, and to assume among the powers of the earth, the separate and equal station to which the Laws of Nature and Nature's God entitle them, a decent respect to the opinions of mankind requires that they should declare the causes which impel them to the separation.

We hold these truths to be self-evident, that all men are created equal, that they are endowed by their Creator with certain unalienable rights; that among these are Life, Liberty, and the pursuit of Happiness. —That, to secure these rights, Governments are instituted among Men, deriving their just powers from the consent of the governed, —That, whenever any Form of Government becomes destructive of these ends, it is the Right of the People to alter or to abolish it, and to institute a new Government, laying its foundation on such principles, and organizing its powers in such form, as to them shall seem most likely to effect their Safety and Happiness. Prudence, indeed, will dictate that Governments long established should not be changed for light and transient causes; and accordingly all experience hath shewn, that mankind are more disposed to suffer, while evils are sufferable, than to right themselves by abolishing the forms to which they are accustomed. But when a long train of abuses and usurpations, pursuing invariable the same Object, evinces a design to reduce them under absolute despotism, it is their right, it is their duty, to throw off such Government, and to provide new guards for their future security.

Black Panther Party Office, Harlem

BO HOLMSTRÖM, REPORTER: This is the Harlem office where the twenty-one Panthers who are now on trial worked. But despite the arrests, political education is still being carried out here today—regular classes in revolution. As most of the men are in jail, the teachers are predominantly female. That's how the revolution in America is being carried out. They're reading the Panthers' paper and having discussions.

BLACK PANTHER WOMAN: No, we're making a revolution by educating the people to the fact that they should arm themselves in self-defense, you see. Educate them to what the power structure is doing to them, that they made racism the primary objective that the people have to deal with, when we mainly have to deal with capitalism. The more we intensify the struggle, you are going to see more and more of them start killing us, because they got too many of us in jail now. And they don't want no more of us in jail, so they got to kill us.

It's not fun having all these people in jail, but these are freedom fighters. They are the vanguards and they are here to liberate the people and they know they either have to go to jail or die. And if you're not prepared for that, then you don't belong in the Black Panther Party.

Kathleen Cleaver, 2010

The Black Panther Party started in Oakland, California. The party is known mostly for its confrontational stances. And that is a good thing, to be confrontational against evil and violence. The kind of problems that the Black communities suffer: unequal levels of imprisonment, unequal levels of access to resources, poor health. So the Black Panther Party did try to model for the community some of the possible solutions that were not capitalist-oriented, like free clinics. You could come here to get free medical care or send your children to us; we will feed them for free. And this idea of free breakfast is one of the legacies that's been adopted. Now the schools have free breakfast, but they didn't before. I think the Party was not the only organization that did it, but it's the only organization based in ghetto communities that did it.

Bobby Seale in Stockholm, Sweden, 1968.

Below:
Kathleen Cleaver in Algiers, Algeria, 1972.

Eldridge Cleaver, Algeria, 1969

KNUT STÅHLBERG: On the highest point in el-Biar in Algiers, among the finest villas, we find Eldridge Cleaver and the Black Panther Party headquarters. The villa has been put at their disposal by the Algerian government. Cleaver, his wife Kathleen, and maybe twenty other Panthers are in the care of the Algerian government. But Cleaver is in exile. The goal seems so remote, and you get the feeling that the spring within him is a bit broken.
CLEAVER: According to my observations, and depending upon how the struggle develops, the next stage is to achieve what the South Vietnamese have achieved. That is, a provisional government, a government that's not in full control of its territory, that does not enjoy its full sovereignty, but which is recognized on a full diplomatic level by sympathetic governments and people around the world. Of course we realize we are a far stage away from that, but the status that we have achieved enables us to function.

Bobby Seale, Stockholm, Sweden, 1969

Bobby Seale was, with Huey P. Newton, one of the founders of the Black Panther Party and its longtime chairman. He was imprisoned several times for his Party activism. Today he is still an activist in the Black community and serves as a community liaison with the African American Studies department at Temple University in Philadelphia.

RAIJA LOUNAVAARA, REPORTER: Bobby Seale says that the Black Panthers are an American revolutionary party working to fulfill the basic needs of the Black population—work, food, housing, and education—and teaching the community how to protect itself against police brutality. Despite what's often said, the Black Panthers do work together with white radical and revolutionary organizations.
SEALE: We look at this program as a very international-type program. It's for any human beings who want to survive.
LOUNAVAARA: It's a plain socialist program?
SEALE: Definitely socialism is the order of the day and not Nixon's Black capitalism, that's out.
LOUNAVAARA: The Black Panthers is an armed organization. What does that mean?
SEALE: It means that if any racist dogs, policemen, or pigs come up and attack

us at any point, we will defend ourselves; we will shoot them, we will kill them, because we are bent on surviving.

LOUNAVAARA: And you have arms to do this?

SEALE: Definitely. And we'll try to get as many arms as we can, and we are teaching the people themselves in the community to arm themselves.

Bobby Seale, Oakland, California, 2010

I wanted some grassroots-up power to the people. Legislation and laws that gave the grassroots real empowerment, you know what I mean? What I believed in was, how do we get greater community control and community input into the political institutions that affect our lives. The very philosophy and slogan that we're spouting is: All power to all the people. Whether you're white, Black, blue, red, green, yellow, or polka dot, in the final analysis, we want real people's community control and empowerment.

Robin D. G. Kelley, 2010

Robin D. G. Kelley is an author and historian of African American social movements and culture. He is the Gary B. Nash Professor of American History at the University of California, Los Angeles.

I mean this is a period when America's empire really takes off; besides the war in Vietnam, there are all these other kinds of interventions. Between 1964 and 1972 there are three hundred urban rebellions in cities, sixty thousand people arrested, billions of dollars' worth of property damage, 250 people killed. Almost all these instances were caused by some police violence, police brutality, and if you're looking from the outside in, I don't care if you're in Beijing, you're in New Delhi, or you're in Malmö, you're going to see America with this internal war. It looks like a racist war.

1970

Huey P. Newton

(1942–1989)

“USA, Murderer!
USA, Murderer!”

Chant at demonstration in Stockholm, Sweden, 1970

The New York 21

BO HOLMSTRÖM: Political trials are getting more and more common in the USA. In Chicago, we have been following the trials of seven leaders of radical parties. They are accused of planning to start riots at the Democratic National Convention. It's a trial that is less about a crime and more about the political views of the society of the accused. And now the same thing has started here in New York.

GERALD B. LEFCOURT, LAWYER: Yes, it's a political trial, we told the judge that. When you take militant Black Panthers, who have been created by a system of oppression and you bring them into a courtroom, you are creating a political trial. Added to it, of course, is the severe punishment that they've already suffered, waiting almost one year for trial in jail conditions that are certainly from the Middle Ages.

REPORTER: But it's a crime case, with bombs and things?

LEFCOURT: Yes, that's the criminal charge. But that's almost being lost in the midst of the political fury.

REPORTER: But in your defense you pressed the political points?

LEFCOURT: I have to present my clients' views toward society: I see that as my role as an attorney. If that is a part of the case, and if it's a relevant part of the case, we will introduce it.

REPORTER: When a defendant stands up and shouts and calls the judge a pig, what happens legally?

LEFCOURT: Legally, he pays a contempt-of-court fine and could be sent to jail for contempt.

REPORTER: Do they know it?

LEFCOURT: Sure they know it. We all told them. But they are facing so many years now that it doesn't seem to matter to them.

Outside, people are demonstrating in sympathy for the twenty-one Black Panthers accused of bombing different places in New York. Not many can get into the courtroom. The line is long. Everyone is body-searched for weapons.

Cameras are forbidden. Artist Claes Folcker's pencil is the only thing allowed to capture what's happening. Most of the spectators are other Black Panthers, women and mothers, and a few whites, who get yelled at by the Blacks already outside the courtroom.

"You only came here to see a Black man get hanged!" a Black woman shouts at some white spectators.

It seems like a fistfight is close. When sixteen of the twenty-one enter, the court room is overfilled. Policemen line the walls. The accused rise, raising clenched fists to the audience. In unison everyone is shouting: "All power to the people!"—the slogan of the Panthers. There is nobody who doesn't get it. They think it's a political trial. This is the establishment's way of smashing the Panther Party.

There are many lawyers. Nobody gets paid. They do it for the sake of the cause. And maybe for the sake of publicity. The judge is a racist, the audience says. "He has spoken critically toward the Panthers. He was handpicked for this mission," they say. And according to his behavior, they seem to be right. The prosecutor gets to finish. The lawyers are silenced and threatened by the judge. It's implied by the judge that the lawyers will have to pay for all the tumult in court.

A police officer takes the witness stand. He was the one who arrested some of the Panthers in their homes. He also confiscated posters from their walls with images of Panthers leaders and a portrait of Mao Tse-tung.

LAWYER: Why did you take the poster?

POLICEMAN: Evidence. It's evidence of conspiracy.

LAWYER: Are you married with kids?

POLICEMAN: Yes.

LAWYER: Where do you live?

The prosecutor jumps up in objection. The defense lawyer objects to the objection. The prosecutor interrupts him, takes the posters from the lawyer's desk, holds them in his hands. The lawyer objects, of course. The prosecutor interrupts him yet again. The lawyer yells, "Could you shut up until I'm finished?" He receives a reprimand from the judge. The audience protests.

LAWYER: Are you living in Harlem?

The judge interrupts. The accused jump up and scream: "The judge is a white pig! No policemen should ever live in Harlem. They know nothing about Harlem. They just come in to kill us."

The courtroom is rocking from the response of the crowd, as the Panthers' own "Right on" rings through the room. The judge commands the Panthers to shut up. Instead they rise and shout: "You have kept Blacks silenced for several hundred years. Now we won't be silenced until we're freed."

"Right on!" from the crowd. A white woman stands and yells: "Injustice!"

The judge orders the guards to throw her out. The entire courtroom is in an uproar. The accused Panthers strike and wound a policeman. The trial is adjourned—for the umpteenth time.

When it's continued, Lefcourt cross-examines the policeman and uncovers, with a few questions, everything the Panthers claim: the police are looking to kill them.

LAWYER: How do you regard the Panther Party?
POLICEMAN: It is a terrorist organization.
LAWYER: Did you say that the Panthers should be eliminated?
POLICEMAN: Yes!
LAWYER: Have you said this to officers under your command?
POLICEMAN: Yes.
LAWYER: Should they be shot to death?
POLICEMAN: Not necessarily.

The courtroom explodes again. Clenched fists in the air. The Panthers scream: "He did say it! We heard it! Kill the police! Kill the pig. Right on! All power to the people."

Robin D. G. Kelley, 2010

For me to have lived through this and seen this through my young eyes in the late sixties and seventies, but then to see it all through the eyes of a Swedish crew, it's even more fascinating because there is a sense of innocence that I think is evident. Yet it's not really innocence as much as it is also a global perspective that's pretty extraordinary. There's simply no way to predict that this revolution will come to an end. What will be next?

Gerald B. Lefcourt, lawyer for the New York 21.

Below:
A supporter rallies outside the courthouse.

Angela Davis, 2010

I can remember that I hoped to organize a massive protest against the invasion of Cambodia in the spring of 1970. I was teaching at UCLA at that time, and there were many of us who wanted to include the attack on the Black Panther Party in the protest. Because this was the period of time when Black Panther Party offices throughout the country were being subject to attack, after J. Edgar Hoover had announced that the Black Panther Party was the greatest threat to American security, so we felt that it was really important to bring these two issues together. The US military was responsible for violence in Vietnam and violence in Cambodia and violence in Southeast Asia in general. And the police departments, under the leadership of the US government and J. Edgar Hoover, were attacking the offices of the Black Panther Party throughout the country.

There was an attack in LA, there was one in New York, in Chicago where Fred Hampton and Mark Clark were killed. And so I remember very clearly how we were attempting to craft a movement that would allow people to understand the interconnections between that state violence. State violence in the form of imperialism against the people of Southeast Asia and state violence against Black people and people who were struggling against racism and for equality at home. We were somewhat successful, but not as successful as I would have liked to have been. It took many years before people began to understand that it's okay to address multiple issues simultaneously. And, as a matter of fact, we can be much more effective if we understand the connections. We bring more people together, we create a greater sense of solidarity, and we move forward with the struggle for justice.

Huey P. Newton, Oakland, California, 1970

Huey Newton overcame an impoverished childhood in segregated Louisiana to educate himself and become, with Bobby Seale, a founder of the Black Panther Party. He was arrested in 1968, accused of shooting a police officer, and spent two years in prison. He was freed after an international campaign, spearheaded by Kathleen Cleaver, rallied to his defense.

ÖRJAN ÖBERG, REPORTER: This is Huey Newton, the founder and leader of the Black Panthers, on his way out of his trial in Oakland, California. This is the fourth time his trial has been postponed. Huey Newton has been bailed out for a sum of fifty thousand dollars.

A number of trials against radicals are being carried out across the country: the trial against Bobby Seale; the trial against the Black intellectual Angela Davis; and the trial against prominent Panthers in New York. The information minister of the Panthers, Eldridge Cleaver, is in exile in Algeria.

The only free leader of the Panthers is now Huey P. Newton. The verdict of manslaughter against him was unjust. He was unconscious at the time of the murder.

NEWTON: I spent a period of three years in California State Prison. During that three years I was kept in solitary confinement for a period of twenty-one hours a day. I was allowed to come out for breakfast, lunch, and dinner, and then I was placed again in this solitary confinement cell. I wasn't allowed to read literature, including literature inside of the prison library. I wasn't allowed to have toothpaste, deodorant, or any of the toilet articles that most people use as a necessity. My treatment was generally abusive and oppressive, primarily because of the fact I was a prisoner of war and a political prisoner.

REPORTER: What do you think is going to happen with the Black Panthers now, losing your leaders, et cetera?

NEWTON: It is true that many of our leaders have been confined in the concentration camps here in America. The American government, the ruling circle, call these concentration camps "rehabilitation centers," but in fact they are no different than any other internment camp that is used for prisoners of war and political prisoners. I know that the Black Panther Party will prevail; it is the vanguard of the people's struggle. And that while leaders are

put into prison, new leaders are born, new leaders are made, because the leaders of the Party come from the people.
VOICEOVER: In addition to free school breakfasts and lunches, the Black Panthers run free health clinics and free legal services to help the poor against the police, landlords and social welfare authorities. It has also been a program of free clothes and the defense of political prisoners. Party members are receiving weapons training and medical education.

BOY: Free Bobby, you hear me, everybody out there free Bobby!
TEACHER 1: Why do we want to free Bobby?
TEACHER 2: Right on!

NEWTON: We feed many thousands of children per day. All of our programs are repeated in every community. In other words, we have forty-four branches and chapters. We attempt to establish institutions, or as we call them, community centers, clothing distribution, breakfast-for-children program. We just opened up, or we are opening up, we have the machinery for, a shoe factory, where we will give free shoes to the children. We will gain the money, we will acquire the money to buy the leather through sales of our newspapers.
REPORTER: Are there only Black kids in the breakfast program?
NEWTON: No, any child is welcomed without discrimination and without categorizing them in any way. We are not bureaucrats; they don't have to fill out applications, so we don't even know their family backgrounds. We know that our program is not—all of our programs, our breakfast-for-children programs, our free-clothing program, our shoe factory, our busing-parents-to-prisons program, our transportation for the old-aged to the hospitals—we know that these are not revolutionary programs. They are at best survival programs. We know that the people are in jeopardy of genocide, and if they don't survive, then it won't be possible to bring about a revolution.
TEACHER: Michelle, name the three points.
MICHELLE: Okay, number one means obey all orders and all your actions. It means don't question your orders, because if a pig get ready to whack you and you be running around and talking about how and what, then you will be killed. And number two, don't take single piece of thread from the poor people, the masses. Which means don't take anything from the poor man, because they don't have anything to start with. And number three, turning everything in that you captured, like a pig or a gun from a pig or some money,

Above:
Huey P. Newton
leaving jail.

Below:
A Black Panther Party
button worn by
a supporter.

turn it in where you ought to turn it in.

TEACHER: Right on.

GIRL 2: Any Party member shouldn't do narcotics and will be expelled from the party. You're not supposed to. . .

TEACHER: Explain that book, the book on your desks. There is a needle in this dude's hand and he is shooting it somewhere—

GIRL 2: He's shooting it in his arm. You're not supposed to shoot up some junk or anything. These pigs been giving people narcotics because pigs want to see the people dead. And the Black Panther Party is trying teach the people not to use this stuff.

TEACHER: If there was fifteen pigs in the community and a brother shot eight of them, how many of them is left?

BOY: Seven.

TEACHER: Seven what?

BOY: Seven more pigs left.

TEACHER: And what are you going to do with those seven more pigs left?

BOY: Kill them.

TEACHER: Right on.

REPORTER: What is the purpose of the liberation school?

NEWTON: The establishment schools are racist, reactionary, bureaucratic, and they tend to miseducate. Our children do not learn how to read in the public schools, I didn't learn how to read in a public school. I taught myself to read after I graduated from high school, so I was around sixteen years old before I could read very simple words. And this is what we work to avoid, this catastrophe, this tragedy. So therefore we have instructors who are very qualified, who have teaching credentials from the establishment schools but now are teaching our children. And we have emphasized the science of reading, writing, and 'rithmetic. And also we teach the kids about the new world that they must create. We teach many children around our forty-four chapters or branches, of roughly forty to fifty children in each school.

REPORTER: You don't try to educate them in hatred?

NEWTON: No. We educate them in the American history, in the American society, and in the treachery of the ruling circle. Sometimes that history is very dreary, that history is very bleak, and so we attempt to give them the true history, without coloring it, without euphemism or attempting to show it the way it is not.

CHILDREN CHANTING:
We want land, bread, housing, education,
clothing, justice, and peace.
And as our major political objective,
a United Nations–supervised plebiscite
to be held throughout the Black colony
in which only Black colonial subjects will be allowed to participate
for the purpose of determining the will of Black people
as to their national destiny.

Huey P. Newton, 1970

When the party was formed in October 1966, we felt it necessary to be Black nationalists. Shortly after that, we saw that we could not gain our liberation through establishing a separate state, because we only represented, as a racial group or ethnic group, 11 percent of the people here in North America. Because of this realization we started to think in terms of uniting with other people who were struggling for freedom, against the same enemy—the small ruling clique that lived in the empire of America.

We called ourselves, then, revolutionary nationalists. But shortly after that we realized that nation-states—there were many wars that been fought for national liberation, that were not based upon socialist principles, and these wars of national liberation seemed to negate themselves or fail. So we reevaluated our position, and we found that it was necessary not to be nationalists at all, but internationalists. Nations ceased to exist when the ruling circle of the United States became imperialist, when America became an empire.

They control not only their own economy but they extend their economical ram and also their political ram. And this is why the United States' ruling circle will not recognize wars any longer. They call it police actions when they send out their troops. They handle everything as a domestic disturbance. In fact, the ruling circle calls Vietnam nothing more than a riot—and they must establish peace again. At one time in history it wasn't enough to be separated ten thousand, fifteen thousand miles, wasn't sufficient to declare yourself a nation of independent people.

At this time the world is very small because of the developments in technology, of satellite TV, where the fascist Nixon would speak on TV

Children in the Black Panther Party's Free Breakfast Program, Oakland, 1971.

from Washington and people would hear him at that minute all over the world. So as far as the separation, it is clear that would not qualify people for nationhood. Some other people will consider another quality that used to qualify people as a nation as their culture or their ethnic background, or their history that happens to be different than some other people's history. At this time the United States' ruling circle are attempting to transform the cultures of the world. I think Japan is a good example. We call the people of the world a disparate collection of communities under siege. We say: our communities exist, nations do not, and the nations more resemble communities. Communities, by way of definition, are a comprehensive collection of institutions that are supposed to serve the people. After all the people of the world liberate their communities and there is a redistribution of wealth on a world level, of course we think in a way of communism, because that's the qualities of communism.

One world community, one economy, and the withering away of the state. The state is already withering away in a reactionary manner with the ruling circle controlling all of the community, so now we want a revolutionary in the communities. This is the cry of the people's vanguards, the Black Panther Party, and this is the only way we are able to free our chairman, Bobby Seale, and Angela, and the Soledad Brothers, all political prisoners.

1971

Elaine Brown
(1943–)

“The whole realm of jails and prisons is something people don’t want to look at, don’t want to be bothered with. It’s a kind of a nightmare which they tuck away somewhere.”

—*Angela Davis*

Attica

LARS HELANDER, REPORTER: The US is the country getting the most attention on Swedish TV at the moment. But is Swedish TV portraying a distorted image of America? Is Swedish TV anti-American? The USA's biggest magazine, *TV Guide*, claims this in a recent article. The editor in chief, Merrill Panitt, wrote the article after a visit to Europe. The criticism was mostly against Holland and Sweden. Apparently Sweden was the worst.
PANITT: The only thing I was interested in when I was there was the Swedish television coverage of America and American news. That I did criticize, because I felt that there was a general anti-American feeling.
REPORTER: How would you define the concept of anti-Americanism?
PANITT: I would define it as emphasizing only the negative aspects of America and none of the positive ones. [*He smiles.*]
VOICEOVER: The following are some of the quotes from the article in *TV Guide*: "The most unrestrained anti-American television this side of the Iron Curtain comes from Sweden."
SWEDISH TV ANCHOR: During this weekend American B-52 planes have dropped a thousand tons of bombs.
VOICEOVER: "Swedish TV is portraying America as an evil country run by evil men. Already, negative news from America is edited to an even more negative viewpoint. Swedish media has the most hostile viewpoint against America."
PANITT: But you see that we are seeing the bad news about America on our own television in the context of living here, of seeing about us every day the positive aspects, so that we have a more realistic perspective of what's going on in America. Whereas the people in Sweden, people abroad, are not living in America, do not see any of the positive aspects of it, and are

getting just the bad news. And this is the thing that I'm objecting to.
REPORTER: I think that one very important factor in this change, because I think there is a change, too, is the war, of course.
PANITT: There's no doubt about that. I'm sure the war is as unpopular here as it is in Sweden, but we're stuck with it. I mean, this is an American problem.

EMILE DE ANTONIO, FILMMAKER: *TV Guide* is an absolute nothing magazine. *TV Guide* is a special kind of magazine that panders to the lowest possible taste in American life. This is one of the reasons it has such a wide circulation. I found it very curious that *TV Guide* should suddenly attack Swedish and Dutch television. And meaningful, deeply meaningful—not in the sense that anybody would believe it—your average reader of *TV Guide* doesn't care about that kind of thing—but only when you consider the threat with the publisher of *TV Guide*, Walter Annenberg, who is the United States' ambassador in London and who is one of Mr. Nixon's closest advisors as well as one of his closest financial supporters.

What I suppose anti-American really means, by and large, at least the way I interpret it—I'm regarded as anti-American. I'm not anti-American; I'm simply against those institutions which rule America. I'm against those institutions which encourage racism, which have put us into the war and kept us in the war. The true picture of what goes on here can even be seen on American television if you look at it long enough: the emptiness, the spiritual bleakness, the loss of meaning, the loss of purpose. The *TV Guide* article on Swedish television is simply a reflection of Mr. Nixon's paranoia.

Attica, New York, 1971

In January 1970, Opie Miller, a sharpshooter at Soledad Prison in California, fired into a crowd of prisoners, killing three Black inmates and wounding one white inmate. In response, thirteen Black inmates began a hunger strike, demanding a federal investigation of the deaths. A judge ruled the killings to be "justifiable homicide." Shortly thereafter, another white guard was found dead. Three of the hunger strikers—George Jackson, Fleeta Drumgo, and John Clutchette—were charged with his murder. They became known as the "Soledad Brothers," a name Jackson, a complex political thinker, used later that year as the title of his collected prison writings, which became a bestseller. The Soledad Brothers became an international cause célèbre, and Angela Davis led their defense campaign. Less than a year later, on August 21, 1971, George Jackson was shot to death by corrections officers in San Quentin Prison. The killing sparked a revolt at Attica Prison in which the prisoners rioted and seized control of the prison.

KNUT STÅHLBERG, REPORTER: The prisoners in Attica revolted and barricaded themselves, with thirty-eight guards as hostages. The prisoners produced a list of thirty demands for better living conditions in exchange for the hostages. The demands were predominantly for more humane treatment: an end to physical abuse, basic necessities like toothbrushes and showers every day. For professional training, and access to newspapers and books. Also demands for transport out of the country to a non-imperialistic nation.

The riot lasted for four days, until the police and National Guardsmen stormed the prison. Forty people were shot dead: thirty-one prisoners and nine of the guards who were held hostage.

It was said immediately that the prisoners cut the guards' throats. But the autopsies showed that all had been shot by the storming troops.

William Kunstler, 1971

Bill Kunstler (1919–1995) was a radical civil rights lawyer who defended the Attica prison rioters, as well as many other figures on the left, including members of the Weather Underground and the American Indian Movement.

KUNSTLER: It's murder under any doctrine of civilized standards that any country ever had.

BO HOLMQVIST, REPORTER: William Kunstler is a radical lawyer. He was in the prison during the revolt, as a member of the observer committee, and tried to negotiate between the prisoners and the authorities. He says now that the governor is guilty of the murders.

KUNSTLER: The prisoners had two non-negotiable demands: the removal of the warden and general amnesty. They had already given up on the removal of the warden. And on the general amnesty, we had worked out several formulas that we were discussing with the commissioner hours before the attack, and if we had been allowed to continue everyone would be alive and the matter would be settled today.

REPORTER: But you yourself said at one point that you feared for your life in there?

Filmmaker Emile de Antonio.

Below:
Lawyer
William Kunstler.

KUNSTLER: Well, I guess I'm a white, middle-class citizen of this country, and I had all the stereotypes about prisoners that any person in my capacity has. I had to learn the hard way that they were decent, honorable men. Much more decent and much more honorable than the people that went in there to shoot them.

John Forté, 2010

John Forté is a violinist and singer who was nominated for a Grammy for his work with the Fugees. He spent eight years in prison for a drug offense, an experience that turned him into an activist.

I think that for a very, very long time, perhaps as long as we've conceived of the concept of prison and what that's supposed to mean, there are some fundamental questions that need to be asked. Is prison about reform and rehabilitation, or is it just about punishment? Depending upon how we address that question, that will ultimately lead to what or how the Attica Rising can be viewed. Because from a human rights perspective, the question comes down to something that's very fundamental. What are prisoners' rights? Do prisoners have human rights?

From the prisoners' position, it was clear that they weren't asking to have any unreasonable freedoms, at least ultimately. I can't look at the Attica Rising without imagining myself there or without taking into account my own experience with prison. And I know that from the inside out, that I never lost my humanity and I never lost my decency. No matter how many times I felt encaged and felt like I was treated in part, perhaps in large part, as an animal, I never lost what it was like to feel like a man and—I felt like I deserved more, in many cases, over the course of my own incarceration. So I can't look at Attica and not sympathize with those prisoners and those inmates who wanted to be treated more decently, for whatever reason. It's a question of dignity and decency.

And to make a mistake is one thing, but to be treated subhumanly, well, that's another. And I think that that was the argument they were attempting to make. We're not being treated fairly on a basic human level. And that deserves, if nothing else, a dialogue. It deserves a discourse. Because no matter what, these are still living and breathing men, and they ought to have that respect, to have that conversation.

One of the first books that I read when I went away was a book by Angela Davis called *Are Prisons Obsolete?* It allowed me to examine

Attica Prison, Attica, New York, 1972.

prisons within America from an institutionalized standpoint, and to examine their history and their role in society. Prior to the Civil War, as Ms. Angela Davis points out in her book, prisons weren't deemed—or I should say Black men in particular weren't deemed good enough for prisons. Prison was too good for them, so you had justice that was carried out on a more violent, more primal level, in the form of lynchings or whippings. That was how justice was carried out. And it was accepted, it was part of the status quo.

Well, then following the Civil War and actually leading into the civil rights movement, it was accepted in many societies to enact these laws that would keep Black people, within America in particular, repressed and oppressed into a life of indentured servitude. So, if we look at it from a purely historical standpoint, leading up to the civil rights movement and Attica, there was nothing that ever happened up until that point where there was such a pivotal change and what was allowed to take place, what was sought through history, leading up to that powder keg, up to the violence that erupted and demanded the world to pay attention. Because it had been happening for so long. So, that's really the importance of what we bear witness to. I wasn't alive then, but just looking at the footage, it's no wonder why there was that eruption—and I'm not saying that the eruption was justified on either side—but you can only put contents under pressure for so long before there is an explosion, and that's just simple physics.

You know, a couple of things have happened since then with the prison system, if we look at and examine the seventies and the eighties with the introduction of the War on Drugs. Systemically, a lot of men and women, instead of being treated like they had issues and addictions with drugs, they were criminalized and their behavior was criminalized. And stiffer penalties weren't handed to the dealers. But what it did was it locked up a significant portion of inner-city populations for an inordinately long period of time. As those populations began increasing in the prison system, the prison complex had to grow with that. So the bureaucracy within that growing system, whether you're talking about the Federal Bureau of Prisons or whether you're talking about state prisons, they had to accommodate these enormous populations. Now what we saw take place was towns and cities across America started receiving more incentives to build prisons. And more incentives to build prisons than incentives to build schools. So this is what is referred to as the prison-industrial complex, where it's really not about reforming, rehabilitation; it's more so about punishment and warehousing.

Are we setting ourselves up for failure by imprisoning a couple of million people and not giving them the tools that they will need to successfully return to society and contribute to society? We have a return rate of 68 percent. Sixty-eight percent of the men and women who come home, within the first three years, will violate the conditions of their probation or their parole. Yes, we can look at a person's responsibility and say: Look, well, these inmates haven't taken the time to use it wisely, to be reformed or to be rehabilitated. Or we can say: Systemically, what sorts of programs are happening or not happening that will cut down on criminal behavior, or that will encourage and inspire people to become productive role models, law-abiding citizens, especially during situations and living with conditions that don't always inspire them to toe the line and to stay within the rules of the law? Because they feel that, for whatever reason, the odds are against them. But, when all that was taken away from us, our freedom, our ability to see our friends, family, and loved ones, we were left with that real desire to prove to ourselves that we weren't animals. So the first law was respect, and we treated each other with respect and with decency—and that was my experience. Perhaps that's not the experience for many. But I would beg anyone to question everything that they've been told about any system just because it might be the plot of your favorite book or your favorite film. And that's why it's easier to have these gross and violent exaggerations about characters and incidents. Because, in some awful way, it allows some people to sleep better at night. And it saddens me.

Black Panther Party headquarters, Oakland, California.

Elaine Brown, Oakland, California, 1971

Elaine Brown served as the Black Panther Party's minister of information and was later its first female chairperson. She remains an activist today.

REPORTER: We are here in the main headquarters of the Black Panthers. It's the main headquarters for the whole of the States?

BROWN: Yes, that's right. Primarily we function here as a center for information and communications throughout the entire party. Which is not only our branches and chapters here in the United States, but also support committees and other friends that we have around the world.

REPORTER: And why do you have this headquarters here in Oakland?

BROWN: Oakland is the place where the Black Panther Party was founded by Huey Newton and Bobby Seale in 1966.

REPORTER: What is the new policy of the Black Panthers now?

BROWN: The policy isn't new. We like to say that we're returning to what we call our "original vision," which was to serve the people and to move the masses of our people, Black and other oppressed people inside of this country, to the point of total liberation. And what that will require, we're willing to engage in. What is new is that we have stopped becoming what we would call a revolutionary cultist group—to, in fact, engage in the work of bringing about the total transformation of the society for the interest and in the interest of the masses of people.

REPORTER: Does that mean you have no guns anymore?

BROWN: Ah, no. What we mean is that the gun, at one time, was looked upon by members of our party—and we put forward this image—that the gun itself was the liberating tool. And what we're trying to explain is that the gun is only a part of the situation. Chairman Bobby, for example, the chairman of our party, will tell you that in order to provide the people with the institutions that they need, to in fact control their communities—for example, a medical clinic—then a gun will not hammer the nails into the walls so that we can build a medical clinic. But a gun will defend the right of the person to have that medical clinic. And so it has to be put in its proper perspective. And so we say that we have the survival programs for the purpose of not only providing people with institutions in their communities, but providing them with the idea of having and controlling their own institutions. And that the gun will always be there, always be ready, to defend the right of the people to have those institutions. In other words, the struggle, the revolution that we're involved in, is not about the gun, it's not about killing people—it's about building things. The gun will always be there to back up our right to do that.

REPORTER: And you have lost many people?

BROWN: Our party itself, of course, in capacity to the number of Black people that have been killed and poor people that have been killed since this country was put together, and since this land was stolen from the people that were here by the Europeans that came—in those four hundred years, of course, there have been millions of Black people killed due to the conditions, due to the political oppression and the economic oppression of this society, and during the period of shackled slavery and so forth. But the number of Black Panther Party members that have been killed since our struggle has developed in this way has been close to forty. Most of the people that have been killed I have known and loved very much, and we miss them very much. I have, for example, attended over fifteen funerals of very beloved people. People that I have loved very dearly.

And so there is this new concept. What we're trying to say is that we're not here trying to build heroic images that people can make posters out of or that they can glorify without understanding. The point is for the struggle to be waged between oppressed people and the oppressor, not between the Black Panther Party and the police. And that was a problem—that, up until now, I think people regarded that the struggle was outside of the people: it only involved the Black Panther Party and the police. And so what we're doing now is extending the struggle and trying to return ourselves to our community and to unify the entire oppressed people so that the struggle between, or the contradiction between, the oppressed and the oppressor can be made clear. And our idea is that, as people begin to see smaller successes, they will want larger and larger successes. And there will be a point at which, we believe, the system will not be able to bend to compromise with the people's demands, and it will be that point at which perhaps the contradiction will reach its head. And perhaps this will eventuate in armed struggle or whatever, but at that point the people will demand the seizure of complete power. And if the government won't compromise that bloodlessly, then perhaps with armed struggle they will.

REPORTER: What do you think about Angela Davis? She is not from the Black Panther Party.

BROWN: No, Angela Davis is a very close friend of the Black Panther Party.

When she was not in jail she was a very strong speaker and she worked very hard on behalf of our Party. And on behalf of, particularly, the freedom of Bobby Seale and Ericka Huggins, who were there in jail in New Haven. And everywhere she would go she would always talk about Bobby, always talk about Ericka. She had the attention of the public at that time and she used that attention to talk about the people who were in jail, in particular. She talked not only about them but also about the Soledad Brothers case, which included of course, George Jackson and the other two brothers, Fleeta Drumgo and John Clutchette. And so Angela became very close to the Party, she was a very good friend of mine and even prior to her being in the Communist Party as she is now, and prior to my being in the Black Panther Party, she's always been a very close and very strong fighter for the people's liberation.

REPORTER: What is the relationship between the Black Panther Party and other political movements?

BROWN: Inside of this country, inside of the United States, our position is that of course we are going to, whenever the occasion rises for specific reasons, then we have good close relationships with most progressive organizations. But our prime interest, of course, is the relationship that we have with the people. And so, generally speaking, we don't get involved in a lot of coalitions with other organizations. If they are working with the people and we think what they're doing is fine, if they're not, then it isn't fine. We don't get into too much theoretical discussion with other groups as to what any of us should do, particularly, because the real response and the real concern would have to come from the people. Our main interest is in the people as opposed to other organizations. And so we don't specifically have a coalition with this organization or that, nor would we not have if the occasion would arise.

1972

Angela Davis

(1944–)

"From the time I was very small, I remember the sounds of bombs exploding across the street, our house shaking. . . . You ask me whether I approve of violence?"

—Angela Davis

Intersectionality

The United States broke diplomatic ties to Sweden after Prime Minister Olof Palme compared the US war in Vietnam to Nazi massacres. Palme made his comments during the Christmas Bombings, during which, from December 18 to 29, 1972, the US Air Force launched the largest heavy bomber strikes since World War II on the city of Hanoi. US B-52 bombers flew more than 750 missions and dropped 20,237 tons of ordnance. Sixteen hundred civilians died in the raids; the North Vietnamese said that the United States had "carpet-bombed hospitals, schools, and residential areas, committing barbarous crimes against our people." Prime Minister Palme appeared on the eight o'clock news to discuss the bombings with Swedish reporters, stating the following:

OLOF PALME: You should call things by their right names. And what is happening today in Vietnam, it is a form of torture. There can be no military justification for bombing of this magnitude. What they are doing now, it's torturing people, plaguing a nation in order to humiliate it, force it into submission by the language of power. Because of this, the bombings are an act of savagery. And of that, we have many examples in modern history. And they are generally associated with a name: Guernica, Oradour, Babi Yar, Katy, Lidice, Sharpeville, Treblinka—here violence has triumphed. But the judgment of the global community has fallen hard over those who bear the responsibility. Now we have added a new name to the row: Hanoi, Christmas 1972.

REPORTER: Does this mean that you then equate the acts that Hitler engaged in, to what President Nixon is now doing?

PALME: I equated the meaningless violence to individuals. It was not the politicians I compared; it is the impact on individuals and the futility of violence and cruelty that I compare.

Marin County Courthouse, California, 1972

BO HOLMSTRÖM: Angela Davis. Her name and face are recognizable from thousands of protests around the world. She's a symbol for the Black struggle against oppression not only in America but in the whole world. Protests have been arranged for her sake in Africa, South America, Europe, and the Soviet Union.

It was here that it all started: Marin County Courthouse in California. On August 7, 1970, James McClain was on trial for allegedly attempting to stab a guard in San Quentin State Prison. Two other Black prisoners were witnesses at the trial. It had nothing to do with Angela Davis. It's not known if they even knew each other. Also in the courtroom sat seventeen-year-old Jonathan Jackson, the younger brother of the Soledad Brother George Jackson, with whom Angela Davis was very close.

Jonathan Jackson stood up and yelled, "Everyone freeze!" and pulled out a gun. He handed weapons to the two Black witnesses and attempted to take a hostage. They never got further than the parking lot, where a shootout with the police took place. The judge, the two Black witnesses, and Jonathan Jackson were killed. The police claimed that Angela Davis was the owner of the gun Jonathan Jackson had used.

Angela Davis went into hiding. Much later, the police found her at a New York hotel. She stands accused as an accomplice to murder, as she was the owner of the gun—a crime punishable by death under California law.

Dennis Roberts and Haywood Burns, Angela Davis's attorneys, spoke to Swedish journalists.

ROBERTS: This trial, I think, will be historic in its unfairness. There is no evidence at all to involve Miss Davis in the charges, none whatsoever. And I think that they seized upon this opportunity to try and put her to death. Governor Reagan originally fired her from her teaching job at University of California and this is simply an extension of that, as far as I'm concerned. The evidence presented to the grand jury shows that the guns that were used in the shootout in San Rafael were registered in her name. Now, assuming for the sake of argument that that's true, that's all it shows, that she owns some guns. There's nothing illegal in the state of California about owning guns. They were registered and it's not a crime. But because of the inflammatory press that had built up around this incident and because of the need that the government felt to put her in jail and to hopefully, from their point of view, to kill her, they could put enough pressure in that grand jury room to get an indictment.

VOICEOVER: No one believes she was behind the murders. She and her thousands of supporters will be sure to politicize her trial. Her defense team is an endless string of lawyers from around America. We met one of them here in Harlem.

BURNS: In fact we question whether—if Angela Davis could get a fair trial anywhere in America, because of the way which the media treated this case, the way in it has been judged already, the way in which the president of the United States has commented upon the case. It's a very political kind of case.

REPORTER: One year in solitary confinement. How is she?

BURNS: Unfortunately, she is not especially well. Spirits are good. But she has lost considerable weight during this one-year period. She has had some damage to her eyesight. I don't know if it's irreparable damage. Although she gets medical attention in the jail, it's not adequate. Physically, she is not in as good condition as we would like. Mentally and spiritually, she is very strong. And it seems that the kind of adversary she's facing makes her that much more strong, that much more committed. So that people that are opposed to change should realize, putting Angela Davis in this kind of situation only makes her tougher, rather than weaker.

BO HOLMSTRÖM, REPORTER: Angela Davis is the symbol of the combined revolutionary and radical movements in the US today. She is a communist. Despite that, she is so admired that the few existing film clips of her speaking are worn out.

Angela Davis is an extraordinary person. Her life has fascinated far more people than just the radicals. All the big newspapers in the US have had big articles on her, saying that she is not from ordinary Black poverty. She played the piano for two years, read poetry for three years. She had brilliant grades in school, with French literature as a major. She has received one of the best educations a Black person in America can get. She also studied in France and Germany, where her professors testified that she was the most gifted student they ever had.

In Germany she met Herbert Marcuse. It was through him that her interest in philosophy and Marxism grew. Her doctoral thesis was on Kant's analysis of the violence in the French Revolution. She's more intelligent and knowledgeable than most people. She has not let the prison stay break her down. She's on a hunger strike as a protest against her treatment. She's Black, she's a woman, and she stands accused of murder. Despite all that, she seems to be a model not only for women but for most Blacks.

> **Angela Davis, 2010**
> In my case, when I think about the fact that Ronald Reagan was the governor of California, Richard Nixon was the president of the US—the whole apparatus of the state was set up against me. They have all the resources, the FBI, the police—they really meant to send me to the death chamber in order to make a point. It really didn't matter who I was; it was that I was a very convenient figure to make a point that they would suppress any efforts at revolution and liberation.

BO HOLMSTRÖM, REPORTER: Very few have met her. She's being detained in this building, a courthouse outside of San Francisco, in a small cell in the basement. Swedish Television demanded, for more than a year, to get an interview with her. We have pushed that requirement through the courts with the help of several lawyers. Finally, we now have a court order that will give us access to a short interview. We have to endure the most rigorous security control we have ever experienced to get in.

Both us and all of our equipment are entirely searched; even the camera is opened and then carefully sealed. There has never been a television interview inside this jail. This is the first time a TV camera has been brought to her cell. She seems silent and pale when we visit her. There are eight people in the room, four of them lawyers; they listen to every word she says, with rigorous juridical rules on what one can and cannot talk about. She has a court order not to say anything about the trial. She is pale and quiet, saying she has medical issues after her time in jail.

DAVIS: I don't think I have very critical medical problems. But I do have something that should be taken care of.

Before I was arrested, I devoted a great deal of my time to the emerging struggle around the prisons. I was led to that by my involvement in the Soledad Brothers Defense Committee. I began as a coordinator of a committee which concerned itself primarily with defending George Jackson,

Demonstrators rally in support of Angela Davis, 1972.

Below:
Angela Davis enters the courtroom.

Bo Holmström reports from outside the San Francisco courthouse where Davis is jailed.

Below:
Angela Davis and Bo Holmström.

Fleeta Drumgo, and John Clutchette against the charges, which we felt where instances of political retaliation. In the process of doing research of what was actually going on around the Soledad Brothers case, we began to realize it was not just a question of having to defend political prisoners who were already in prison, but something was terribly wrong within the prison system. And this, in fact, had to be a central struggle for not only the revolutionaries, not only for radicals, but for all people who really believed that justice is to prevail in this country. There were so many things that I had absolutely no idea of going on in prisons. So I think it sort of generally tends to be the case in almost any society, that the whole realm of jails and prisons is something people don't want to look at, don't want to be bothered with. It's a kind of a nightmare which they tuck away somewhere and do not open themselves up to.

After we discovered that it was not just George Jackson, Fleeta Drumgo, and John Clutchette, it was thousands and thousands of brothers and sisters all over the country who are receiving the same kind of treatment, who are being subjected to the same kind of political punishment, and just basic human rights being violated. For example, men could be placed in a box-like cell, with a cement floor, with a hole to use as a toilet. And no light. And that was it. They could be placed in this cell for up to thirty days. The description of this particular strip cell can actually be found in the transcript of a court case. The things that were going on around the Soledad case are just absolutely unbelievable.

REPORTER: Are violent uprisings like Attica justified to change things like that?

DAVIS: What happened at Attica was that many people in this country and all over the world who had not yet come to be aware of what the situation in prisons actually is had their eyes opened.

REPORTER: And the effect might be change?

DAVIS: I think some degree of change has already occurred. It's interesting: not very long ago, an ex–general attorney, Ramsey Clark, said that he was beginning to believe more and more that prisons had to be abolished. Prisons as we see them now, prisons with their present structure, with their present function in the society.

REPORTER: And some other types of corrections instead?

DAVIS: Yes, precisely. But of course when you talk about corrections, and especially when it relates to Black people, and Chicano, and poor people in general, it's very difficult to talk about a rehabilitation in any kind of authentic sense. Because the real problem is not the fact that a man or a woman has gone out and has taken, stolen, an object here and there. The real problem is that of creating a society where men and women are not forced to resort to those kinds of methods in order to survive.

REPORTER: Would you think that you have a gag order is a problem?

DAVIS: Well, I think that, again, can be traced, in a word, to an attempt to prevent us from being effective in waging our defense. We have a situation where, prior to my arrest, the prosecutor gave numerous interviews to the press, made numerous allegations, discussed numerous things. And then at the date of my arraignment, I'm presented with the court order, which tells me that I can't say anything at all about my case. Of course the reason given for the gag order was that any prejudicial pretrial publicity should not occur, but most of the prejudicial publicity has already transpired.

REPORTER: You will have your chance at the trial to tell your side of the story, won't you?

DAVIS: Well, that's where I am supposed to tell my side of the story, but you have to realize also that, more than likely, the twelve people who will be sitting in the courtroom as jurors have already read all kind of news stories and seen things on television and read magazines and so forth discussing the other side of the case, and that more than likely they would tend to be biased against me not only because—

REPORTER: Do you feel doomed beforehand?

DAVIS: Well, I'm not going to say that I feel doomed, because I think that would be a contradiction to my own political beliefs and my own feeling that the mass struggle is the only thing that is going to bring justice for anyone in this society. I don't feel doomed yet, but still I have to be very realistic about this situation I'm confronting. I have to be realistic about the fact that there will be a very small likelihood that even one Black person will be on the jury.

REPORTER: Is that also to say then that there is no justice to be found for a Black person in the courts in the United States?

DAVIS: Well, I think that wherever justice occurs for Black people in the courts of the United States, it's either an accident or else it's a result of some form of mass struggle. If you look at the statistics of men and women in the prisons, those statistics in themselves tell you that something is terribly wrong. When you have a situation in California where almost 50 percent of the inmate population in the state prison system is Black or Chicano, that tells you that something is terribly wrong.

REPORTER: But on the other hand, we have just heard that the day before yesterday, Huey Newton was freed, the charges dropped after two hung juries. We had Panthers in New York who were acquitted, we had Bobby Seale. . . . This proves that the American justice system works.
DAVIS: Exactly that was said, but when you consider the fact that Bobby Seale and Ericka Huggins spent, well, Ericka spent over two years of her life in prison—over two years—and is that justice? When finally a judge says, well, now you can go free, the New York 21 spent well over two years in prison too, not in prison, prison compared to the Tombs and the jails where the brothers and sisters of New York were being incarcerated is just incredible. I was in the jail where Joan Burden and Afeni Shakur were, and to think that they had to spend two years of their lives under conditions like that, charged with crimes of which they were innocent, and that they couldn't get out because their bail was so high, a hundred thousand dollars per person. I don't see how anyone can say that this is what justice is all about. Does justice mean that anyone in this society, that any person who's a revolutionary, who's a radical activist, can be charged with anything whatsoever and be kept in jail for two years as Huey Newton, as Bobby Seale, and Ericka Huggins, and I can go on, and the list is just indefinite, and then finally they are told that they can go free. Is that what justice is supposed to be?
REPORTER: No, but do you think also that the reason that the bails are so high, or in your case no bail at all, is that because they have political business, are politically active?
DAVIS: There's no doubt about it. You can look at all kinds of records to see that for many years people have been granted bail. Just not too long ago there was this newscaster in Los Angeles who was charged with murder. He was granted bail. Someone in Chicago who was charged with the capital crime of hijacking a plane and killing someone, bail was immediately set. Though they were not communists.
REPORTER: Can you tell me why you are a communist? I don't mean to ask you why you joined that faction, but many other radical people that worked for liberation have not joined the Communist Party in America. Why did you join?
DAVIS: Well, first of all, I have considered myself Marxist for a very long time. As a Black woman, my first commitment is to Black people and to the struggle against racism in this country. However, I feel that it's impossible to talk about the liberation of Black people if one does not, at the same time,

project a revolutionary transformation of all of society, because the problem does not lie with attitude, does not lie with individuals: racism is built into the very structure and fabric of the society, and it is that which has to be completely changed.

REPORTER: You can never see an equal society under a capitalistic system?

DAVIS: I think that is a contradiction in terms; that's such a thing that doesn't exist and can't exist. What you have is the pseudo-kind of political equality, which generally doesn't even exist. Especially when you consider the situation that Black people, you're supposed to be able to be poor but at the same time equal, and it just doesn't work that way.

REPORTER: In this struggle, how do you see the way to liberation except that it can't be under a capitalistic system, which you already said. How is the way to work in a giant capitalistic country like the United States?

DAVIS: How are we to concretely envision socialism, is that what you mean? Well, you see, I think that so many people completely misunderstand what socialism is. That it is all about all of the propaganda that exists. Most people's vision is completely distorted and when you talk about socialism, inevitably, people are asked questions about the Soviet Union or about China or other existing socialist countries. One of the things that should be realized is that socialism in this country would be far different from anything that has ever been seen in the world, because in no other country which experienced the socialist revolution did there exist, concretely, the means and resources of satisfying all of the needs of all the people right now. With all of the fantastic advances that have been made under capitalism, socialism would be something that would appear utopian if we were to think about it now.

REPORTER: Yeah, but the question is, how do you get there? Do you get there by confrontation? Violence?

DAVIS: Oh, is that the question you were asking? You see, that's another thing, when you talk about a revolution most people think violence—without realizing that the real content of any kind of revolutionary thrust lies in the principles, in the goals that you are striving for, not in the way you reach them.

REPORTER: A year ago the Black Panthers were much more active. We heard much more about that type of struggle. Are we in a new time? Has the time of the Black Panthers passed?

DAVIS: The Black Panthers still exist and the Black Panthers are still extremely active in the Oakland community and in communities all over the country. I'm not sure whether you are aware of what is now happening in the Black Panther Party and the kinds of things that members of that party are doing now.

REPORTER: No, but tell me.

DAVIS: Well, there are a number of programs which are well established in the community now. There is a free breakfast program which has been in existence for quite a while, but there are also a number of free medical clinics, free clothing, shoes and a number of things. See, a lot of people don't realize that Black people in this county very often don't have the most rudimentary things you need in order to survive. I remember very clearly in my own childhood that there were a lot of my friends that never had money for lunch. In fact, I would try to take extra money to school so that this sister or this brother could have maybe a bag of potato chips for lunch, they wouldn't starve the whole day. But this is a situation which exists here, and it's not just Mississippi, it's not just Alabama, it's all over the country, in every ghetto. So one of the things that the Black Panther Party was attempting to do now is to see to it that certain basic needs are satisfied. First of all, if you're going to talk about a revolutionary situation, you have to have people who are physically able to wage revolution and are physically able to organize and physically able to do all that is needed to be done.

I think that you are right in a sense when you say there appears to be a much greater emphasis on electoral struggles now. I've been in jail now for well over a year and I don't have any direct contact with what is happening outside. But I feel there's a great deal of confusion in the movement now. Akbar Ahmed made a remark not too long ago that we are like the sons and daughters of widows: we have lost our moorings in the past and have not yet discovered our vision towards the future.

I think that there exists a certain amount of confusion in the movement now; people aren't quite aware of what to do. But among the Black people there exists a very profound consciousness, a political consciousness. Young kids who are growing up know about what's happening. In fact, a rather interesting anecdote involves the young daughter of a Black matron in the jail in New York. The matron told me that her daughter, who was six years old at the time, who attends Catholic school, had been asked to write a small composition on her hero, whom she admired most in America, and she apparently shocked all of the devout Catholics by saying that Bobby Seale was her hero.

I think that you do have a situation in the Black community now where people want change and people seem to have gone a little bit further than just the kinds of demonstrations and protests which have occurred in the past. But yet and still we're not yet prepared and ready to seize power using whatever means is necessary to seize power. On the other hand, because of the way this society is organized, because of the violence that exists on the surface everywhere, you have to expect that there are going to be such explosions, you have to expect things like that as reactions.

If you are a Black person who lives in the Black community all your life and walk out on the streets every day seeing white policemen surrounding you. When I was living in Los Angeles, for instance—long before the situation in LA ever occurred—I was constantly stopped. The police didn't know who I was, but I was a Black woman and I had a natural, and they, I suppose, thought that I might be a, quote, "militant," and so often I'll be stopped, taken out of a car, and frisked. I remember very vividly one situation, during which time I was working with the Black Panther Party, that some members of the Party came to pick me up at a bus station and were going to drive me to the office. They had been followed by the police. And the police stopped us. I was in the car at that point and policeman told the driver, "I'm going to give you a ticket because you didn't stop when you saw the pedestrian who looked like he was getting ready to cross the street," and wrote a ticket. And I was sitting in the backseat next to the window. The man had his hand on his gun, it was unsnapped, and he was so tense—almost shaking—that it was so clear that if anyone in that car had made a false move, somebody would have been hurt or would have been dead.

And when you live under a situation like that constantly and then you ask me, you know, whether I approve of violence, I mean that just doesn't make any sense at all. Whether I approve of guns? I grew up in Birmingham, Alabama, and some very good friends of mine were killed by bombs, bombs that were planted by racists. I remember, from the time I was very small, I remember the sounds of bombs exploding across the street, our house shaking. I remember my father having to have guns at his disposal at all times because of the fact that at any moment someone might expect to be attacked. The man who was at that time in complete control of the city government—his name was Bull Connor—would often get on the radio and make statements like "Niggers have moved into a white neighborhood, we'd better expect some bloodshed tonight," and sure enough, there would be bloodshed.

Angela Davis giving a speech in Madison Square Garden from behind a pane of bulletproof glass after her release from jail.

Below:
Davis leaving captivity, February 23, 1972.

After the four young girls, one of which lived next door to me and I was very good friends with the sister of another one, my sister was very good friends with all three of them, and my mother taught one of them in her class. In fact, when the bombing occurred, one of the mothers of one of the young girls called my mother and said, "Can you take me down to the church to pick up Carol, you know, we heard about the bombing and I don't have my car," and they went down and what did they find? They found limbs and heads strewn all over the place. After that, in my neighborhood, all of the men organized themselves into an armed patrol. They had to take their guns and patrol our community every night because they did not want that to happen again. I mean that's why when somebody asks me about violence, I just find it incredible. Because what it means is that the person that is asking that question has absolutely no idea what Black people have gone through, what Black people have experienced in this country since the time the first Black person was kidnapped from the shores of Africa.

Erykah Badu, 2010

I have to come from where I sit and where I see it. I feel as if I'm standing at an apex looking at everything happening around me and I'm putting myself in this time period. And me being a woman or a right-brained thinker or an emotional being, spiritual being first, human being second, man or woman third, Jew or gentile fourth, pretty or ugly fifth. I see that this time period brought on an evolution and at that time frame, thinking came up out of a pain and a fear. And it appears as if at that time the pain to remain the same outweighed the pain to change. And when that happens, that's the point of destiny where we all must move. And it's contagious like hot coals, one ignites the next, and the next, and the next, it seems as natural as the evolving of this planet. The evolving of our thinking. I see a new world coming and it started long ago. And this period it was more apparent. It was more urgent because we just got tired, and when you get tired enough is when you begin to want to sacrifice everything inside of you, every single thing, and the fear just leaves and this is what's happening in this time period. This is what happens in this time period.

Angela Davis, New York City, 1972

On February 23, 1972, Angela Davis was tried, acquitted, and released after eighteen months of incarceration. After her release from prison, on June 29, she gave a speech at New York's Madison Square Garden—from behind a bulletproof shield.

We say in a thundering, resounding, united voice: We have no intention of stopping this fight until we have eradicated every single remnant of racism in this country. Until we have ended the war in Vietnam and the neocolonialism in Africa. We are not going to stop fighting until every political prisoner is free and until all the monstrous vengeance in this country are mere memories of a nightmare. Sisters and brothers, this is what the power of the people is all about.

Questlove, 2009

To me the worst crime that could ever be committed on mankind is really ignorance. People that don't do anything are perceived just as guilty as those who did something. Americans, especially privileged Americans, are really in denial about what is going on for Black people, for underprivileged people, period, but mainly for Black people. Just because I'm allowed to drink out of the same water fountain or, you know, have a turkey dinner at Walmart's lunch counter doesn't necessarily equal progress or doesn't mean that the wrongs of four hundred years are justified.

Angela Davis, late 1960s

As a communist I have to demand radical change. I see that capitalism is not possessed with flexibility to allow for the solution to the basic problem that confronts us today: exploitation of workers, super-exploitation of Black and brown workers, with high rates of unemployment in our community, bad housing, bad social living conditions, and bad education. I maintain: only under a socialist reorganization of society can we even begin to deal with these basic material problems.

Shirley Chisholm, Brooklyn, New York

Shirley Chisholm (1924–2005) began her career as an educator in Brooklyn. She worked to establish early childhood programs in New York City and ran successfully for the New York State Assembly in 1964. In 1968 she became the first Black woman elected to Congress. On January 25, 1972, she announced her bid for the Democratic presidential nomination.

SHIRLEY CHISHOLM: I stand before you today as a candidate for the Democratic nomination for the presidency of the United States of America. I am not the candidate of Black America, although I am Black and proud. I am not the candidate of the women's movement of this country, although I am a woman and I am equally proud of that. I am not the candidate of any political bosses or fat cats or special interests. I stand here now without endorsement from many big-name politicians or celebrities or any other kind of prop. I am the candidate of the people of America.

VOICEOVER: She is forty-seven, doing her most daring act. Three years ago nobody knew about her. Now Shirley Chisholm is famous all over America. She is the new, sparkling Black leader. She has guts. The word on the street is that she won't live long. They will kill her soon. She was the first Black woman elected to the Congress. She represents Brooklyn, one of the most run-down parts of New York.

CHISHOLM: See little white children with sunken faces, all beyond their years, suffering from malnutrition, hardly able to stand on their two legs in this most affluent society. And then come with me to the Black delta of Mississippi and see little Black children with their stomachs distended, malnutrition. . . . America's children in this most affluent society.

REPORTER: Is it a worse handicap to be a woman? Is it worse than being Black?

CHISHOLM: I find in the field of politics, and I say politics specifically, in the field of politics I have met far more discrimination as a woman than being a Black person in politics.

REPORTER: What kind of reaction did you find when you said that you would run for the presidency, both from the Black and female community, the male white establishment—do they think you are crazy?

CHISHOLM: The male establishment just thought it was one great big joke. Of course, I don't think many of them were terribly surprised at this particular action, because of the fact that they have always understood that Shirley Chisholm was somewhat of a maverick—independent-minded. So I just think that many of them felt, "Oh there she goes again," and they didn't believe that I was really serious. And I think most people—not only men, but, I think, most people—didn't really believe I was serious because of the fact that it takes millions of dollars to run for this office in this country.
REPORTER: Yes, you have no money, do you?
CHISHOLM: Oh, I have relatively small amounts of money, but I have something that many of the other candidates don't have—that you can see here. I have foot soldiers, I have people.
REPORTER: And that is just as great as a lot of the commercials on TV and so forth?
CHISHOLM: Right, but the important thing is to be able to mobilize people, to coordinate to do the job that has to be done. But I have the most important resources in this game, and that's the people. But if we understand the nature of power in our land, we will be able to put together a coalition. A coalition of all of those forces in this country that have never had the opportunity to say anything, absolutely anything, about who is going to guide the ship of state for four years. Namely, the presidency of the United States of America. We need a new voice on the American scene, a voice whose first commitment is to the American people. The poor, the downtrodden, the Indian, the Black, the poor white, the youth, and the women. The multifacetedness of America. They don't want to talk about maybe an Indian running, maybe a Chicano running, maybe a Black running, maybe a woman running. The only thing that matters is that white males must make the determination of everything in this country.
REPORTER: If you were elected, would you be surprised?
CHISHOLM: I guess.
REPORTER: Sometimes when I listen to you I get the feeling that the most important thing is that somebody dared to run.
CHISHOLM: Of course, it's very important that somebody dares to run, to let everybody else in America know that the presidency of this country is not the exclusive domain of just white males. There are all kinds of people that make up America that need to have some input on that highest level. And of course when you're going to break that tradition, you've got to have

"I got a brave heart like the one named Shirley Chisholm"

—A Tribe Called Quest, "Baby Phife's Return," 1996

courage and you've got to have guts and so therefore, because I have always had courage and I have always had guts, I dare to run. It's as simple as that.
REPORTER: Would you be surprised if you were elected?
CHISHOLM: Oh, I don't know if I'd be surprised. I'd have to say the time is long overdue in terms of Blacks' contribution to this country.
REPORTER: Let's imagine you are elected. On your first day in office, what is the most urgent political action you would take? What is the first thing you would do?
CHISHOLM: The first thing, I would change the White House from being called the "White House" and call it the "Polka Dot House." Secondly, my cabinet, my department heads, my agency heads, will be reflective of all kinds of people that make up America. You won't only have white males dominating the departments and the heads of agencies. You'd have women, you'd have Black, you'd have Indians, you'd have Spanish—you'd have, truly, the American dream reflected, that would be the very first thing I would do, because it is my contention that in terms of this coalition candidacy we need many more kinds of Americans in positions of policy and administrative decisions in this country.

[Outside a meeting venue]
REPORTER: Are you a member of the Black Panthers?
MAN: Yes, I'm a member of the Georgia state chapter of the Black Panther Party.
REPORTER: And you support Shirley Chisholm?
MAN: Well, I support anybody that supports the people. Anyone that says that they're gonna represent the people—not racist, like one just for Black,

one just for white, but a supporter of all people. All the presently exploited people.

REPORTER: Do you believe in the process, with election and everything then, do you?

MAN: I don't believe in it, but while it exists, then we have to support the candidates that are put in office to represent the people.

ANOTHER MAN: White man ain't gonna let her be the president, never. If she would become the president, she won't last. We killed Martin Luther King, they just killed the president of the labor union here, a small local union, International Labor Union, he just got killed Sunday. He was nothing more than a local labor union. So what do you think about the president of the United States being Black?

REPORTER: You were guarded by the Black Panthers in Atlanta. Do you need a guard?

CHISHOLM: The Black Panthers understand, in a very long sense, what I'm trying to do. Some of them may have certain little hang-ups, but they know, they understand power—in terms of what I'm trying to do—better than some of the Black male politicians in this country.

REPORTER: So you welcome them?

CHISHOLM: I welcome everybody that wants to support me. America's composed of all kinds of people.

REPORTER: But you need a guard from them. Is it dangerous, this?

CHISHOLM: Well, let's say that I am moving out in terms of running for the very highest office in this land, and because I am a very outspoken kind of person, people who care about me want to help to protect me. And I welcome the protection.

But what do you believe America is composed of? Are we saying an America that only white males are the only ones that have all the brain power, all of the talent, all of the creativity? For fifteen years of my life I have been writing speeches for white males. For fifteen years of my life I have been the interpreter. Racism.

That's why I say to the young of America: I gave up on my generation long ago. I say to you, young people, I mean it: you're going to have to help me and others to change our country, to make it the kind of country that it can be. All of us love America, but many of us do not measure America by her achievements. We measure America by her potential for becoming what she can truly become: truly a haven for all kinds of people, regardless

Shirley Chisholm

of race, creed, or color. That's what I am about, as I go up and down the highways and the byways of this country.

I have a vision just like Martin Luther King had a dream, I have a vision. I have a vision that the powerless and helpless in our country can come together—crossing sex lines, crossing color lines, and even crossing ideological lines. So don't underestimate me. When people say, "Don't waste your vote on Mrs. Chisholm," or "She can't be president," all you say to people is this: even if Mrs. Chisholm cannot be president of this country, Mrs. Chisholm will be able to go to the convention—the first national convention in this country—as an instrument of all kinds of people who never had any input. And she will be bargaining for us at that convention, in order to be able to put together a ticket that is reflective of the total American society. That's how you answer them.

Chisholm knew she would not win the election. She won about 10 percent of the vote in the states where her name was on the ballot—a respectable result for a candidate with a campaign budget of only three hundred thousand dollars. She remained in Congress until 1983.

Despite daily death threats, there was no assault on Chisholm. Ironically, her opponent on the other side of the political field, George Wallace, was gunned down; he survived but was paralyzed. The politician character in the film *Taxi Driver* is inspired by him and this incident.

"Reagan is the prez but I voted for Shirley Chisholm"

—Biz Markie, "Nobody Beats the Biz," 1988

"Clinton is the president I still voted for Shirley Chisholm"

—Redman and Method Man, "Maaaad Crew," 1999

"You're the prism Shirley Chisholm was the first"

—Outkast, "Spread," 2003

ATIONAL CITY BANK

1973

Lewis H. Michaux

(1885–1976)

"Black is beautiful but Black isn't power, knowledge is power. For you can be Black as a crow, you can be white as snow, and if you don't know and ain't got no dough you can't go, and that's for sho'."

—*Lewis H. Michaux*

Lewis H. Michaux
Harlem, 1973

Lewis Michaux (1885–1976) was a writer and activist who owned the African National Memorial Bookstore on Seventh Avenue in Harlem during the forties and fifties. He entertained intellectuals and African political leaders—Langston Hughes and Marcus Garvey were regular customers—and Malcolm X and others spoke in front of his store. His customers called him "the Professor," even though his formal education was minimal. He was an inspiration and a mentor to many young students.

LEWIS H. MICHAUX: And now you're standing in the place of the largest collection of Black books in the world. And that started off some forty years ago in this place, me sleeping in the cellar. My receipts each day were around a dollar and a quarter, but I don't tell how much my receipts are today, or Internal Revenue will be looking for me! Seventy-five percent of these books are concentrating on Black. To give the youth of today some dignity, and the heritage of where they are from, their homeland. Africa is the Black man's home. It's not a bookstore—to me this is an institution of learning, this is wonderful.

Malcolm X was the smartest uneducated. You see, Malcolm X, they could find nobody with no degree of PhD could debate him on truth. And naturally, this country can't stand truth.

Now, I was lecturing the other day down in the same cellar, and a gang of little Black boys came in and they held up their fists talking about Black Power. I said, "Look, son, I'd like to straighten you out," I said. "Black is beautiful but Black isn't power, knowledge is power. For you can be Black as a crow, you can be white as snow, and if you don't know and ain't got no dough you can't go, and that's for sho'."

And what we are trying to do is to show the young Black youth that's in

America today, that we—not necessarily now—want to go back to Africa. We are going to set up a Watergate! We have a claim on this country for bringing us here, against our will, and working our foreparents to build this great empire. And today we have a claim, but we must get an education to know how to ask for what to do. The white man that landed here, he came with two great weapons. One was the Bible and the other was the gun. If they didn't humble you with the Bible, they'd crumble you with the gun. And they're still praising the Lord and passing ammunition all over the world.

Talib Kweli, 2010

Everything about who I am comes from growing up in Brooklyn and comes from my parents; they laid the foundations. But a big part of why I've been able to touch the world through my music and express myself has to do with the years I spent in a Black bookstore. I mean, this store in Harlem looks identical to Inquire Books that I worked at. The book titles, I know all those books, I've read all those books. And it's interesting that that stuff was still relevant to me when I was working there in the nineties, as relevant as it was in the seventies, because the issues are still the same.

I think is very important because even in Inquire, when I worked there, all the Black businesses in Brooklyn downtown got together and put signs that said "Support Black businesses." Because Amazon.com and all these things was coming up, Barnes and Noble was trying to set up an independent bookstore, and we wanted people to understand that you have to support your Black businesses. You spend a dollar in the Jewish community and it might touch thirty people before it leaves that community. If you spend a dollar in a Black community, it leaves the community immediately. So it's important that we support stores like this.

And a point he said about Black Power that I think is very important—you have to grow and change. You can't just be caught up in the racial aspect of it. You have to, he said in the little poem, he said, you have to know and you have to have the dough you know, you can't just be caught up in, or do it just because your heart is Black. So it's interesting that he ran a Black bookstore. He understood the importance of the bookstore. But he also understood it's not just about the Black. That's the tool, that's not the goal.

Display at the African National Memorial Bookstore in Harlem, New York.

Below:
Lewis H. Michaux.

Harlem, 1973.

Harry Belafonte, 2010

I passed that bookstore at least four times a week. It's wonderful that we have it; it's a repository of many, not all but many, documents that have been printed and put at our disposal in efforts to document and to capture aspects of Black history, of the Black evolution—but it sits there on a small corner in a community. Most Black homes would not have any of those books in them. Most schools, if not all, across America will have none of those books in them. As a matter of fact, in the state of Texas, which publishes the largest number of public school books, books containing instructions in the curriculum have been seriously altered to take out of the books the image of the progressive philosophers and the noble warriors who fought to make America the true democracy we have all dreamed about. And they have in turn said we must praise those who are the leaders of the rebellion against the freedom of the slaves. You most honor equally the Confederate Army and the philosophy of the South. You must say there is no evolution, it's a man-made device to overrule the power of the Bible and God and the Christian Right. All of these things are at play, so when you show this, you show what is wonderful that we have in the community. What's a great tragedy is that we don't have it in every home.

Robin D. G. Kelley, 2010

That footage is amazing. That is amazing. There are no other interviews with Lewis Michaux. Actually, I grew up in that bookstore! My mother used to take us there all the time. I remember, in front of his bookstore, there were always people peddling pamphlets, from the Nation of Islam to various revolutionary organizations. And in those days, especially in the early seventies, there was an identification with the Third World, you know. So it wasn't just Black Power: it was Latin America, it was China, it was, you know, a period of Black-Asian and Black-Latino solidarity. And these are the things that people talk about. And of course Vietnam was important.

I've actually never seen that much footage with Lewis Michaux talking about the project of his bookstore. And I guess one other thing he reminded me of, which is often forgotten: it was a period of reading. Where everyone was reading. So you had your heroin addicts, you had hustlers, you had a certain gang violence and that sort of thing.

But everyone seemed to be reading something. And even had a book. The fact that you had a community reading literature, proclaiming revolution—no matter where it's from, reading Fanon, *The Wretched of the Earth*, reading Richard Wright, and reading poetry like Sonia Sanchez, people like that, it's incredible.

Courtney Callender, Harlem, 1973

Courtney Callender (1937–1983) was New York City's first African American deputy commissioner of cultural affairs. He graduated from New York's prestigious Stuyvesant High School in 1955, attended Howard University in Washington, DC, for one year, and completed his education at the City College of New York, graduating in 1959. There is a playground named after him in New York City. He spoke with Swedish journalists at the Studio Museum in Harlem.

This whole kind of falling in love with Black things for a short period of time is essentially racist. It's hypothesized on a great sense of separateness and a sense of treating Black activities as a kind of curiosity, either benign or threatening, one or the other. When it's threatening, you know, "Oh my God, they're going to riot or something!" And when it's being nice: "Let's let them paint or draw or sing or dance, whatever they want to do, until we get tired of them, till we—the white community—get tired of it." And that whole structure is essentially racist.

CITY OF NEW YORK
POLICE

1974

“There’s no unity
in the world.
You couldn’t rally
five hundred people
to sincerely fight
for the same
common cause,
no matter what that
cause might be,
unless it’s dollars.”

—*Unidentified Harlem doctor, 1974*

Harlem, 1974

[A bus full of Swedish tourists.]

TOUR GUIDE: We're getting closer to the neighborhood known as Harlem. This is undoubtedly the Black man's ghetto. Large amounts of narcotics are circulating in Harlem. So you're constantly trying to raise money to get your fix. You might have read our welcome letter, where we inform you that we do not want anyone to visit Harlem for personal studies. It's because this neighborhood is only for Black people. Not even the better—if I may use that wording—the better colored people visit this area because of the risk of being mugged.

[Inside a police car.]

COP: See, this block is business as usual. Instead of a hundred junkies out today, there must be a thousand out. We say, ride up 127th Street and see the pros, see if we got any new faces working. That's us, pops, let's go. Ladies of the night.

[An unidentified Black doctor spoke with Swedish journalists in a Harlem hospital.]

DOCTOR: Most of our violence is spontaneous. And I think it's mostly stabbings and bloodyings of one sort or another. It has gotten very sophisticated in the last three, four years, and everybody is carrying a gun. When you come to work, you say, am I gonna win tonight? It's your battle against theirs. You start on unequal footing, and maybe they get ahead of you. And you are overwhelmed by these stretcher cases, gunshots, stabbings and overdoses, and whatever you want. Death is so final, so "gone in a minute." I'm frustrated all the time. I don't know how sensitive I am, but still can be

Swedish tourists
in Harlem, 1973.

frustrated about what I see and wonder when it will end and if it ever will end. I'm frustrated by Whitey's contributions. These contributions are usually drugs. It brings to me youngsters of my race. Young people, this is why it's so frustrating—these are preteenagers, thirteen to fifteen. Beautiful specimens, dead from an overdose, and we see this too often. I have to be frank with you, this is something I don't discuss very much. But I know why I am here. I want to make some kind of contribution to this hospital, because it's mine. I was practically born three streets up from here. And I just can't see giving it over to anybody.

John Forté, 2010

To name something a war on anything—so, to call this a War on Drugs, it evokes a very, very violent image for everyone participating. By the mere name alone, you think of what comes with war: the violence, the casualties, the explosions, the pain, the grief, the suffering. The indefiniteness. The messiness of it all. This is not targeted, precise warfare. This is like, I don't know, it's ugly, exactly, this is a war. If you are on the other side of the war you are an enemy combatant. And enemy combatants can be dealt with however the powers that be feel it might be appropriate.

Indeed, the War on Drugs swept everyone up. Whether you were the dealer, whether you were the user, whether you were the friend driving in the car. In so many cases, you could have just been affiliated and implicated by mere proximity in this war. And the numbers speak for themselves. As the Black population comprises 13 percent of the total population of American citizens, yet 49 percent—almost 50 percent—of the prison population. The vast majority of those cases are not violent, but they are drug-related. It begs the question: who is failing whom?

DEALER: You know how many guys out here like me selling dope? You know how many kilograms of dope coming to United States? You know how many times it's handled and how many get a cut of that money? Everyone is selling dope, from the government on down. You don't cut off the hand that feeds you. So in other words, if that's where I'm getting dope from, should I tell and cut off my neck?

VETERAN: I'm twenty-seven years old and I can remember back to 1966 when I first went into the United States Army. Now, they have brothers overseas that don't even know about heroin, and they come overseas with the fact of being a good soldier—you know, doing for the country—but they have no country. And they go over there and they get hooked. I think they wanted it this way, you know, because so many brothers died, it's a shame, and they be lying about the fact. They'll be lying, they'll be saying, "Your son died in combat." He didn't die in combat. He died from an overdose. And as you can see in the papers, everybody's involved, big people involved, they can't break it open.

Angela Davis, 2010
We were aware of some of the collateral consequences of the war in Vietnam, including the fact that young men who fought there—who were drafted, by the way—returned with serious drug problems. And that was the beginning of the period of massive drug problems in the Black communities. The government was involved in some way, the CIA was involved with the distribution of drugs. Drugs were responsible for the receding of militancy and revolutionary impulses in Black communities all over the country.

UNIDENTIFIED BLACK DOCTOR 2: I look out on the world and I see people who have lost their awareness of being committed to any kind of cause at all. There's no unity in the world. You couldn't rally five hundred people to sincerely fight for the same common cause, no matter what that cause might be, unless it's dollars. The result of this is, of course, the chaos that we live in. I fight drug addiction in Harlem, I run the addicts' rehabilitation center. It's a tragedy that we live in a society that believes that it can do everything, that it can go to the moon, and yet it does not believe that it can cure a drug victim of a malady that the society has caused. That's a disgrace.

Malcolm X, radio interview, 1965

The Black people here in Harlem are more intellectually independent than Black people anywhere in America. Black people in Harlem can think for themselves. And Black people in Harlem think Black. Black people in New York they think Black, they walk Black, they talk Black, they're proud to be Black.

A young member of the Nation of Islam, Harlem, 1973.

Below:
Louis Farrakhan

Talib Kweli, 2010

Well, Harlem is romanticized for the culture, and Harlem is different now that it has been gentrified a few times over. So you have influences and money in Harlem that wasn't there, but you still have this. Rich, famous people live there, but right there on the corner they're still selling crack, they're still selling heroin, there are still these same traps. Harlem is a complete metaphor for the Black experience in America.

Louis Farrakhan, 1974

Louis Farrakhan was born in the Bronx as Louis Eugene Wolcott. He was appointed to lead the Nation of Islam (NOI), a Black nationalist Muslim organization, after the death of its leader Elijah Muhammad. His strictly structured, religious Black nationalism was a pole of attraction for many African Americans, and his relationship with former NOI leader Malcolm X was a complicated one. Farrakhan now leads a revived version of the Nation of Islam and received national attention in 1995 when he led the Million Man March.

I am Louis Farrakhan, minister of Muhammad's Temple number 7 in New York City and the national spokesman for the honorable Elijah Muhammad and the Nation of Islam.

The honorable Elijah Muhammad teaches us that almighty God, Allah, revealed to him that the white race is a race of devils—"devil" meaning wicked by nature. What more could a devil do than what has been done to the Black man of America? In theology we have been taught that the devil would get you after you were dead, if you were bad, and you would go to hell, a place of eternal fire, and there the devil would torment us. Well, in that sense, that's a pretty merciful theology—because at least when you go to hell and meet the devil you are dead, and being dead, you're not able to feel pain. Now we are in a literal hell in America.

We do not smoke, we do not drink, we do not use needles or drugs, we do not commit fornication or adultery, we do not gamble, we do not lie, cheat, or steal. We are forbidden even to argue with one another much less fight or draw each other's blood. It is against the very laws of Islam and the law of nature for us to be lazy and sit around waiting and begging somebody else to do for us what we could do for ourselves.

And one thing that I failed to mention a moment ago: that filthy swine.

God has divinely prohibited, through the time of Moses, that man should eat the swine. If you just think for a moment of that ugly creature, that filthy creature, and what the swine eats—how in the world could an intelligent man go and eat that which eats his garbage, eats dung?

Robin D. G. Kelley, 2010

This is a very significant interview because 1974 is about the time when Louis Farrakhan basically made a bid for leadership of what becomes the Nation of Islam. It was a moment when the Nation of Islam itself was full of corruption, internal violence, and assassinations, full of thuggery in some ways. Louis Farrakhan's stature rose significantly at this period. Even in '74, those inside the Nation of Islam and those who had continued to work with the Malcolm Organization of Afro-American Unity had never trusted Farrakhan. They were convinced that he was involved in the assassination. And so what Farrakhan ends up doing is playing down that part. He stops vilifying Malcolm X. Malcolm X dead is more useful to him than alive.

There is a generation of people who are seeking precisely that kind of discipline because the drugs are taking over. The mid-seventies is a period of the beginning of the decline. The violence is taking over, the handguns made available cheaply. Crime is going up. Farrakhan wasn't interested in a political agenda. It was against the rules at the Nation of Islam to adopt a political agenda. It's not until, really, 1980 that you begin to see the Nation of Islam under Farrakhan's leadership becoming more politically active.

Talib Kweli, 2010

I mean, yeah, you know the sixties was very revolutionary in some thoughts and in terms of imagery, Black is beautiful, we love ourselves. And it's documented, it's not even a myth or anything—that is, a conspiracy theory—that the community was flooded with drugs in order to stop these things. I mean Hoover and the FBI, they made sure that the drugs were an influence in the community and it certainly had its effects, just how drugs affect your brain, they affected the community and made everything out of focus. Everything fuzzy. The drugs almost had a renaissance when they did the same thing with crack. It was heroin then, it was crack after that, but that's, you know, people who are poor and oppressed, they focus on survival. The drugs seem like an easy escape route.

LOUIS FARRAKHAN: It is not our hands that will bring about the fall of America. It is the divine power of almighty God, Allah, that is now bringing about the destruction of the United States of America. Her destruction will serve as a warning to all of Europe that America, in her bold mistreatment of the very people of God, is now reaping what she has sown. The same divine plagues that God sent against the Pharaohs in Egypt are now visible in America.

Brooklyn, 1974

VOICEOVER: A brand new baby, but he's already a heroin addict. He was on heroin for nine months before he was born because his mother is a junkie. He has all the symptoms: he has fits, he won't eat, and he never stops crying. He'll have to go through withdrawal, cold turkey. Then? Nobody knows for sure. But he may not grow up as fast as other boys. He could suffer permanent brain damage, and chances are good that he'll end up in a foster home with no mother, no father, nothing. But his own life, some life.

Swedish journalists Lars Ulvenstam and Tomas Dillén spoke with a young woman who worked in the sex trade. She asked to remain anonymous.

YOUNG WOMAN: I used to steal from my mother. I used to do things I really didn't want to do. I have family problems. My stepfather asked me out. That's something I'm holding in, and I could never come up and tell my mother know that her husband asked me to go out. That's something I had to hold in.

The easiest thing I knew how to do was to prostitute myself. I used to go up on Prospect Avenue and hang out on the corners up there till somebody come along and whistle for drivers as they come by. They used to call me over. I used to get in. I used to say, "You want a blowjob?" You know, sometimes they take me to the hotel and I get down with them. I didn't want to do it, but it's something that I had to do.

I got down with them for about five, six dollars. Then find out it wasn't enough. Had to do it constantly about ten men just to get thirty dollars. And I couldn't care who it was, you know, it didn't make me no difference who

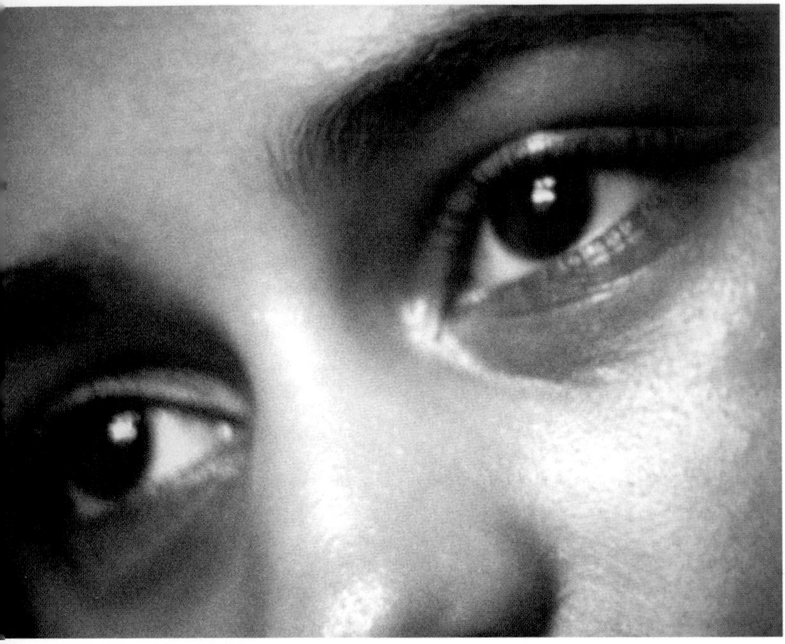

Unidentified girl, Brooklyn, 1973.

it was or where he came from, as long as he had a couple of dollars to give me. My little sisters, they wouldn't respect me, you know, they would be embarrassed to walk down the street with me. I had no self-confidence.

Now still I wasn't ready to come in, because I was doing dope. I kept shooting. I liked it because it feels like when I was high off heroin, I could talk to people, you know. I could party with other people. I didn't have to stay in the house, watch TV, go to bed, get up. I hanged out all night, wouldn't go to sleep. At the time I liked what I was doing. I don't know why, until I got hooked on it. Then I had to get it. I was doing things I didn't want to do. Now I'm just trying to make it now. I think I can make it.

Angela Davis, 2010

What's very sad, it's so sad, is the fact that this young woman in the seventies could explain so eloquently, almost, what her problems were. Especially with respect to drugs, it's a reflection on what we should know now. And, of course, today there is an assumption that there is some kind of cultural poverty—that people are poor because there's some kind of natural force deeming that they should be poor. That the government or the society has no responsibility in this poverty, in driving people to do drugs or find ways to escape what otherwise is a completely dead-end life.

It's just very sad to see that these are things that we should know now, thirty, forty years later, and we should have been able to move beyond this situation. There ought to be drug programs that aren't—to be opportunities, so that people don't find themselves in a situation where drugs are the only way to experience some kind of happiness. Because I think this is what this young woman was saying: that she had no idea what the drugs were doing to her, but she was able to feel better. She obviously did not have a sense of vision for the future or education, participation in a kind of community or collective movement for freedom.

I think we're confronting some of the very same problems today. And here we are in the beginning of the twenty-first century, and we still have not figured out how to provide treatment to drug addicts. And, as a matter of fact, when one looks on the population of people imprisoned today, the population has risen to the point of 2.3 million people behind bars. And substantial numbers of those people who are in prison are in that situation because of the impact of drugs. As a matter of fact, something like 80 percent of all women who are imprisoned now are in on drug-related charges. Something else that I've found really troubling, having worked inside jails, with young people who know about life and who oftentimes make a decision that they want to get off drugs—but there are no facilities available. There's no assistance available. And I can remember talking to a number of young women who said that the only alternative they had was to commit a crime so that they would be sentenced to jail and hope then that they would be deflected to a drug program. And so it's just very sad that thirty years later, forty years later, we are in an even worse situation, I believe, than the one that was described in this clip.

Joan Little, Raleigh, North Carolina, 1974

Joan Little was the first woman in US history to be acquitted using the defense that she used deadly force to resist sexual assault. She was in custody in Beaufort County Jail in North Carolina on August 27, 1974, when a police officer delivering a drunken prisoner discovered the body of jailer Clarence Alligood, 62, on Joan Little's bunk, naked from the waist down. Alligood had suffered stab wounds to the temple and the heart area from an ice pick. Semen was discovered on his leg. Little was missing. She turned herself in to North Carolina authorities more than a week later, saying that she had killed Alligood while defending herself against sexual assault. She was charged with first-degree murder, which carried an automatic death sentence. The capital status of the case, and the fact that North Carolina was home to over one-third of all the death penalty cases in the United States, made the case a major touchpoint for public attention.

SVEN STRÖMBERG, REPORTER: Every morning Joan Little is taken to the court in Raleigh under strict surveillance. She has, several times, been threatened with death by anonymous people. The case, and the attention around Joan Little, has created strong reactions, not only here in North Carolina but in the whole USA. Joan Little has become the unifying symbol for the civil rights movement and other radical organizations right now. Racism, discrimination, and oppression of women are the keywords.

REPORTER: Can you tell me, what are your feelings here? How do you look upon this case?

An addict prepares a dose of heroin.

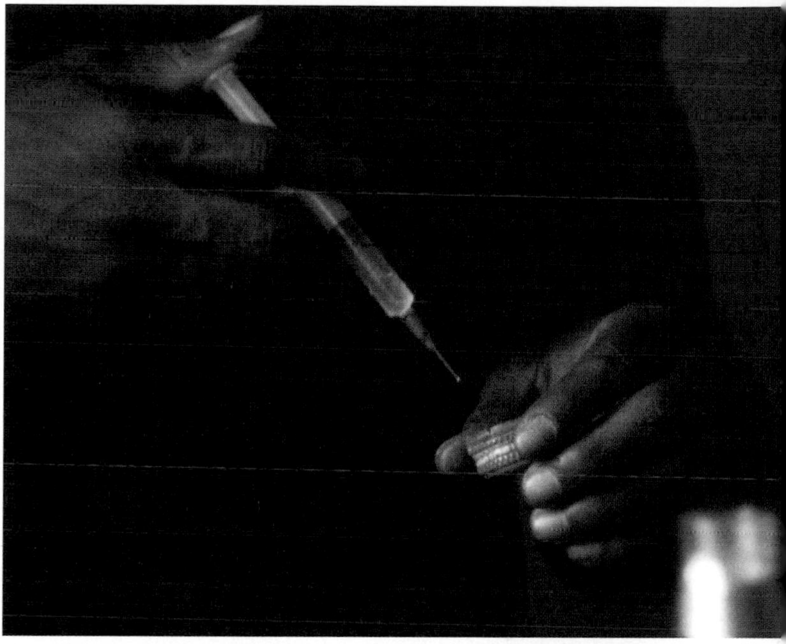

Below:
A baby born addicted to heroin.

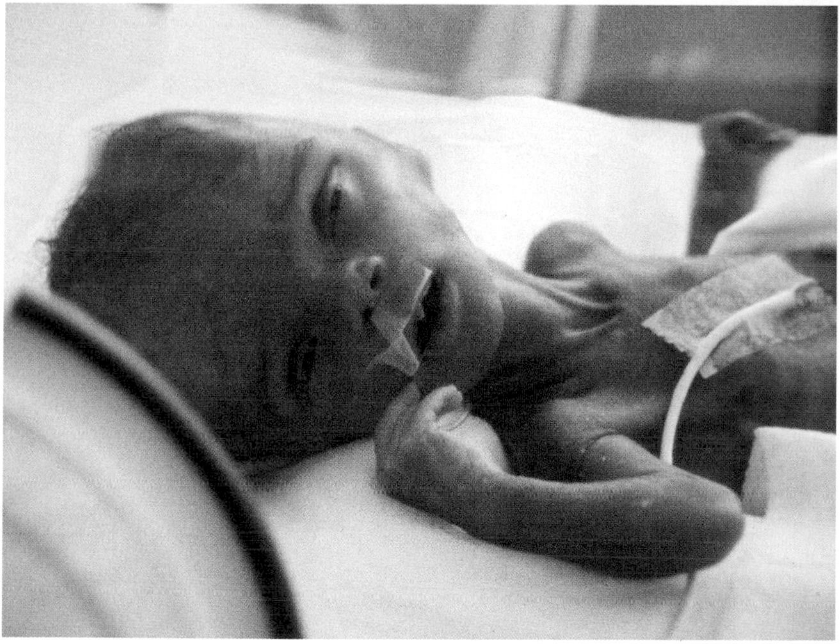

EM

LOYMENT
SILVER RI
NOW
JOBS

LARRY LITTLE, RELATIVE: I think this is one of the most significant cases concerning any Black person in the last thirty or forty years in the history of the United States. We feel it is so important because it goes to the very heart of the question as to whether or not a Black woman has the right to defend herself when she is the victim of a white racist, sexist attack. We feel Joan Little acted in self-defense. And we feel that the way this question is answered will have tremendous repercussions throughout this country, in regards to the life Black women are able to live. For centuries, since Black people were brought to this country, we have more or less been treated as nothing more than a huddle of slaves. And we feel now that white men have in fact taken liberties with Black women and raped Black women, and nothing has ever been done about it. White men have always been exonerated. But when Black men have raped white women, they have gone to death row. Witness the situation in North Carolina, with 80 percent of all people on death row being Black. And so we feel that this case is tremendously important, and we feel that the attention it is receiving is well deserved. The only thing we are hoping for now is that Joan Little be exonerated, that she's found to be innocent. And this will be a new day for Black women in America.

VOICEOVER: This is the jury that will decide Joan Little's destiny. The primary alternative is the death penalty or acquittal of the charges of premeditated murder. They also need to consider the principal questions, like what human rights does a prisoner have in a prison in America today? Especially a Black prisoner—and in addition, a woman, deserted and sexually abused. The composition of the jury is surprisingly liberal. Five are Black. Several are women. There are seven lawyers on the defense side and many civil rights lawyers to help Joan Little after a nationwide collection. The hope is that this trial will become a good forum to illuminate these problems.

REPORTER: Do you think this is a good case to prove this sort of things?
MARWIN MILLER, ATTORNEY: I think so. I think all these things are combined in one case. There have been individual cases involving different aspects, but not the whole combination, such as this one; this involves all these at one time.
REPORTER: How do you look upon the American system of justice generally, when you compare this case?
MILLER: Generally the American system of justice is pretty much a failure,

to a large degree. This case may turn out, and we feel will turn out, to be a victory for Joan Little, but even if Joan Little wins her case, that doesn't vindicate the American system of justice. Because Joan is a poor person, she doesn't have a lot of money, and the only way that she would have been able to win this case would be that a lot of people have donated a lot of money and a lot of time. Poor people just can't amass a defense like this. These kinds of cases are happening across the country every day, all the time. And one case that gets in the limelight where things go right doesn't mean that the whole system works.

VOICEOVER: The judge's name is Hamilton H. Hobgood. He has been a criminal judge for twenty-seven years. His colleagues say he's incorruptibly hard. He has effectively prevented the politicization of opinions. It was also the judge who moved the trial from Joan Little's hometown and this environment. The chances for Joan to have a fair trial would be small here. It was here Joan was convicted the first time. The prisoner's guard was an honorable man, says the white majority. The prosecutor, who is here from Washington, DC, is being assisted by a former Ku Klux Klan member. He is a strong advocate for the death penalty. The same goes for the attorney general in Washington, DC, William Mayo. But he doesn't like the accusations of discrimination and the attention from the media.

WILLIAM MAYO: Well, we watched the news. And of course it bothers us a great deal. And I do not feel that we are those types of people that we been portrayed as in the news. People here generally have a tendency to live together happily, both white and the colored citizens. And the only difficulties we've had here is when outside people come in and have a tendency to want to disrupt what has been a normal, friendly course to living together. I feel like so many of our people, both Black and white, are happy here. And over the past years many of our colored citizens have moved away, and in time we find that many of them are moving back. Because they are unhappy where they have moved to in the northern states and they want to come back home.

VOICEOVER: Joan Little grew up in the slum here in Washington, North Carolina. Her background speaks against her. She was placed in a community home, convicted for shoplifting several times, and was convicted, after a strange trial, and sent to prison last year for theft. It was for that she had been detained when she escaped in August and her prison guard was found dead, half-naked in her cell.

Joan Little supporters, North Carolina, 1975.

Below:
Joan Little at the police station, North Carolina, 1975.

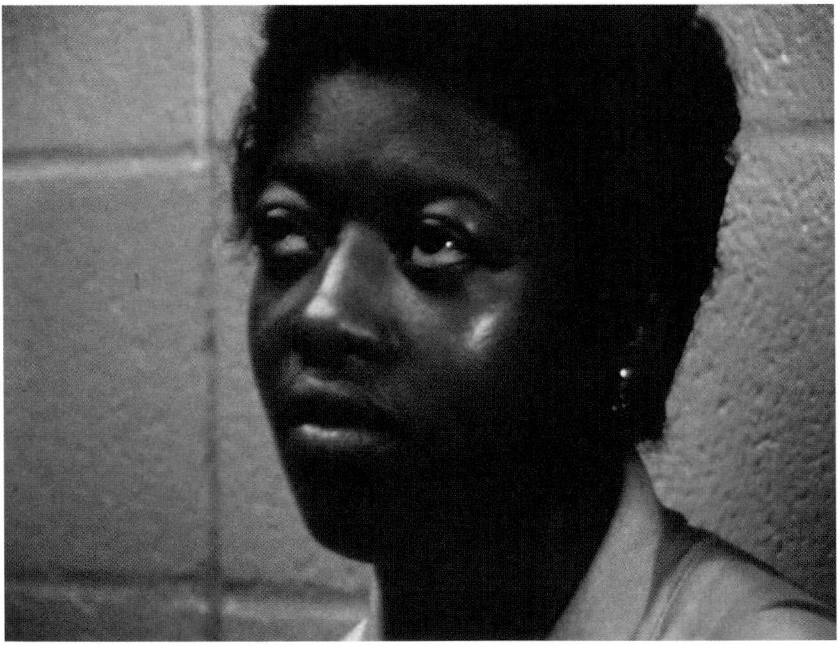

Joan hid herself in Washington and found a group that believed her when she said she had acted in self-defense and that she could no longer take the sexual abuse. Her case is now the hope for many Blacks for an improvement of the legal system and justice, even though they still look pessimistic on the situation.

JOHN COLEMAN, SOCIAL WORKER: I don't know if it could change anything. At least it brings awareness, which I think is good. Because I think more people have to become aware of what the system is all about, how it works, who it works for, who it does not work for. Okay, you say justice for all, supposedly in the United States, but I think the mere fact that you all are here, that the case itself has brought about worldwide attention, which I think is good, tells you something else. I would like to say it would change something, change the system itself. But factually and realistically, I just don't know. I hope it does.

ANGELA DAVIS: Joan Little was like so many other hundreds of thousands of Black people who get railroaded into prison and caught in that whole machine of juridical oppression because they are poor, they aren't able to afford good lawyers, and because of the racism of the judge and the racism of the of jurisdiction system.

Angela Davis, 2010

DAVIS: During the time I was in jail, there was a massive campaign organized around the demand for my freedom. I welcomed that support, of course, because it meant in a very real way that my life was saved by people all over the world who stood up for my freedom. However, I also felt that I didn't deserve to be the only person who benefited from this solidarity and these organized protests all over. During the time I was in jail, the name of the committee that coordinated the campaign for my freedom was changed from the National United Community to Free Angela Davis to the National Committee to Free Angela Davis and All Political Prisoners.

And so, immediately after I was released, thanks to the work of so many people—including people in Sweden—I eventually traveled to Sweden, and I was able to directly express my gratitude to people there who had been involved in the campaign for my freedom. But immediately afterward, we began to organize a new group that would not only address political prisoners but that would also look at prisoners' rights—that would begin to address the role of the prison system and that would look at racist formations such as the Ku Klux Klan. And this organization was called the National Alliance Against Racist and Political Repression.

One of the first major efforts we undertook was a campaign in North Carolina. At that time Reverend Ben Davies, who became a prominent figure in the United Church of Christ, was in jail. There were many other political prisoners in North Carolina. There were many people on death row, so we did this North Carolina campaign. Now, in North Carolina, there was a young woman by the name of Joan Little who had been charged with the killing of a jail guard. And we took on her case. I became very active in her case. It was also for me a way to think about the intersections of racism and sexism and state violence. And so we argued that Joan Little was being punished because she defended herself against rape. And as we know now, rape and sexual abuse abound in prisons, especially in women's prisons. So here was a situation where a prison guard had forced himself on her with an ice pick, had used an ice pick to force her to submit to rape, and when she—after he had completed the sexual assault—grabbed the ice pick and stabbed him, she was the one charged with murder.

We did an enormous campaign around her case and as a result of the involvement of many different people, people who were involved in the Black movement, people involved in the movement for the freedom of political prisoners, feminists who were beginning to take up the question of rape got involved and the outcome of the trial was very positive. One, she was actually found not guilty, and it was a precedent-setting campaign, I think.

OLSSON: Do you think that Joan Little being freed of the charges was the fruit of all the labors and sacrifices you and others had made for ten years before that?

DAVIS: Well, I think it was definitely related to that movement. And, you know, we were able to call upon people. The Black people were involved, as I said before. The feminist movement that was just beginning to develop became a source of support. I wrote an article that appeared in Gloria Steinem's magazine, *Ms.*, and quite a few people responded to that. So it was a very powerful moment.

It was important not only because it resulted in the acquittal of Joan Little but also because it demonstrated what we could do if we could only come together. If we could recognize that somehow differences did not mean we could not work together. And that working on different issues didn't mean we couldn't discover the connections and the intersections in the way in which they were crosshatched, you know, overlaying, so it was a powerful moment. It was an absolutely incredible campaign.

I went to visit her in jail, and I did work with her lawyer Jerry Paul, and I helped to prepare the defense. I was, at that time, doing work; I had published an article, when I was in jail, on the role of Black women in the community of slaves. And I had made some arguments about the political role of sexual assault under the condition of slavery. And so some of these arguments I refashioned and recrafted, so that they could be used in the defense. So I had an opportunity to talk to Joan about these things and to work very closely with her and her lawyer during the course of the trial.

I appreciated the fact that Joan Little was someone who, although she had not been political before, did not resist the development of a political movement around her case. And of course, you know, when you decide to defend particular individuals, you can't determine who those individuals are or what they are going to turn out to be. There were some problems afterward. And Joan Little was never a person who became intensely political, but I think she recognized how important it was not only for her own future but for the women's movement and the Black movement to organize around her case.

1975

"We serv
PAN

The People'
her

“Many of us do not measure America by her achievements. We measure America by her potential for becoming what she can truly become: truly a haven for all kinds of people, regardless of race, creed, or color.”

—Shirley Chisholm

A Better World

Erykah Badu, 2010

Sometimes I feel like there's a lot of rebuilding in order, and a lot of that is going to come from just the old-fashioned principle of reading books. More importantly, we have to write and document our history right now. It's really not about Black and white. It's about the story that we're going to tell. Let's tell the story right—so that's why we as Black people have to tell our own stories. We have to document our history because when we allow someone else to document our history, the history becomes twisted and we get written out. We get our noses blown off.

Robin D. G. Kelley, 2010

I think of the Black Power movement—see, I always think of it as three different movements, three different legacies. The most evident is this idea of building Black institutions—buying Black and supporting Black businesses, but not necessarily transforming or revolutionizing the society. Nowadays it's manifesting in slogans like "The color of Black Power is green." It's about making money and supporting our businesses. It's not a revolutionary ideology.

Another extreme in that is a kind of cultural nationalism, and it goes in ebbs and flows. When Spike Lee's film *Malcolm X* came out, it was the height of a kind of cultural nationalism. Sort of a resurrection. And then, finally, the other element is the Black radical tradition, which is a tradition of struggle and organization. And how does it exist today? It certainly exists in forms of hip-hop.

You can actually chart both the organizational forms and rhetoric of Black Power in second-wave feminism and in the gay liberation movement.

Where the gay liberation movement, post-Stonewall—in New York but also in San Francisco—in many ways adopted the language of Black Power, gay power, feminist power.

Kenny Gamble, 2009

Kenny Gamble is a songwriter and record producer and a pioneer of Philadelphia soul. He holds a seat in the Rock and Roll Hall of Fame.

This was a great movement in Black America because of the historical aspect of people of African descent here in the United States of America. It's been a tremendous ride here, since slavery and since all of this Ku Klux Klan and all of this madness in this country. So the Black man in America has been able to survive all this and has been able to express themselves through music and art, and been able to utilize the government here and the rules, the regulations, the Constitution and Declaration of Independence, and utilize this in a nonviolent way, to be part of one of the greatest countries that has ever been: the United States of America.

In my opinion, America, during those times of slavery, during those times of Jim Crow and hanging people because they might look on a white woman, all this was madness, in my view. And I think in America, the mentality of people during that time, they were like infants, they were like little babies, and so I think America today has grown up a little bit. Through the civil rights movement, through Billy Paul doing "Am I Black Enough for You," James Brown, "I'm Black and I'm Proud," and Curtis Mayfield, all of his great music. I think America has become maybe a teenager now. And hopefully, in the years to come, America will become an adult. And it will be able to think like an adult and do things like an adult. Right now America is stumbling all over itself, because it's like a teenager.

It's a great concept: every divergent group in the world is here, it's a wonderful thing. And somehow this country, with all different groups of people, they get along with each other and they become Americans. So the key of it is that you must protect the concept and ideals of America, of freedom. This is America, and it's a great concept of freedom of speech, freedom of religion. I mean, chill out, take it easy, try not to put pressure on people. It's a great, great concept, it's not a country, it's not a place, it's a great concept—it just happens to be here in North America

Black Panther Party, Harlem.

that it's being expressed. I'm all for Americanism, I really am. And I think just the good people have to get together in the world and make it what they think, instead of sitting back and watching bad things happen.

Sonia Sanchez, 2010

There's not a day that I don't get up and thank a Stokely and a Malcolm and a Kathleen and an Angela, who did this very hard work for us to begin to not only see the country but to see ourselves and to love ourselves. When you love yourself, you don't want to hurt someone else. And the other thing is, when you love yourself, you treat people as an equal.

Angela Davis, 2010

I think the story about my trial is an important story, and we can talk about others, about Bobby Seale and Ericka Huggins and Huey Newton, and go on and on. The real import of the positive outcome of these trials is that they demonstrated that people can collectively generate the kind of power that can be earth-shaking, that can change lives, that can change societies. People need to know that, particularly in the twenty-first century, it is important—even under a Black president—to bring the kind of pressure, to force the kinds of issues, that will allow us to imagine a future without war and without racism and without prisons.

Sonia Sanchez, 2010

If you look at the world, my dear brother, you can wake up, you can say, "I don't want to get up out of bed." Because, I mean, the rich are getting richer not only in America but around the world. Young people got to see it. I mean sometimes a lot of the young people who are in their forties now say, "I'm tired." I say, "You can't be tired. Take a rest, take a vacation, but this is a lifetime job." We got to talk about that 1 percent or 5 percent that runs everything, you know? It's a lot of work. And you don't get any rewards. You don't really get a reward. But the point is that the reward is knowing when you make a transition, when you die, if you have children, there's a better world for them. And if you don't have children, there's a better world for other people, too.

Tony Miller, soundman and filmmaker.

Below: Demonstration in support of the New York 21.

Urban decay in the Bronx, 1970s.

Photo Credits

Cover:
Angela Davis, by Tom Goetz

Introduction
8: The Panther Party's Free Breakfast Program, Oakland, 1971, by Birchman/Tjernberg/Turai
16: Woman in the Black Panther office, Harlem, 1972, by Anders Ribbsjö
20–21, 22, 23: Hallandale, Florida, 1972, by Michael Kinmanson
25 (top): Dan Holmberg; (bottom): Michael Kinmanson

1967
26–27: Harlem, 1973, by Anders Ribbsjö
28–29, 37, 43, 45: by Lars Hjelm

1968
48–49: The Arizona desert, by Lars Hellengren
50–51, 59, 62, 65, 66: Photo credits not listed in archive file
69: by Lars Hellengren

1969
72–73: San Francisco, by Birchman/Tjernberg/Turai
74–75: by Birchman/Tjernberg/Turai
81: Huey P. Newton leaving jail, by Michael Kinmanson
82, 85 (top): by Birchman/Tjernberg/Turai
85 (bottom): Photo credit not listed in archive file

1970
88–89: Harlem, 1973, by Anders Ribbsjö
90–91: by Dan Holmberg
97: Photo credits not listed in archive file
101 (top): Huey P. Newton leaving jail, by Michael Kinmanson
101 (bottom)–104: by Birchman/Tjernberg/Turai

1971

106–7: Still from *The Year of the Pig*, photographer unknown
108–9: Photo credit not listed in archive file
115 (top): by Åke Åstrand
115 (bottom): by Dan Holmberg
117, 120: by Tom Goetz

1972

124–25: Angela Davis being arrested in New York City,
photo credit not listed in archive file
126–27: by Tom Goetz
134, 135 (top): Photo credits not listed in archive file
135 (bottom), 142 (top): by Tom Goetz
142 (bottom), 146–47, 151 (top): Photo credit not listed in archive file
151 (bottom): by Tom Goetz

1973

154–55: by Tom Goetz
156–57, 162–63, 165, 166–67, 168–69, 173, 176, 180, 183: by Anders Ribbsjö
184–85: Photographer unknown

1974

188 (top): by Anders Ribbsjö
188 (bottom): Photo credit not listed in archive file

1975

192–93: Statue of Liberty, photo credit not listed in archive file
194–95: Black Panther Party office, photo credit not listed in archive file
200, 202 (top): by Anders Ribbsjö
202 (bottom): by Michael Kinmanson
203 (top): by Anders Ribbsjö
203 (bottom): by Dan Holmberg

Index of Names

About Haymarket Books

Haymarket Books is a nonprofit, progressive book distributor and publisher, a project of the Center for Economic Research and Social Change. We believe that activists need to take ideas, history, and politics into the many struggles for social justice today. Learning the lessons of past victories, as well as defeats, can arm a new generation of fighters for a better world. As Karl Marx said, "The philosophers have merely interpreted the world; the point however is to change it."

We take inspiration and courage from our namesakes, the Haymarket Martyrs, who gave their lives fighting for a better world. Their 1886 struggle for the eight-hour day, which gave us May Day, the international workers' holiday, reminds workers around the world that ordinary people can organize and struggle for their own liberation. These struggles continue today across the globe—struggles against oppression, exploitation, hunger, and poverty.

It was August Spies, one of the Martyrs who was targeted for being an immigrant and an anarchist, who predicted the battles being fought to this day. "If you think that by hanging us you can stamp out the labor movement," Spies told the judge, "then hang us. Here you will tread upon a spark, but here, and there, and behind you, and in front of you, and everywhere, the flames will blaze up. It is a subterranean fire. You cannot put it out. The ground is on fire upon which you stand."

We could not succeed in our publishing efforts without the generous financial support of our readers. Many people contribute to our project through the Haymarket Sustainers program, where donors receive free books in return for their monetary support. If you would like to be a part of this program, please contact us at info@haymarketbooks.org.

HaymarketBooks.org